FREE TIME

FREE TIME

Making Your Leisure Count

JAN L. GAULT, Ph.D.
Uptime, San Francisco, CA.

Illustration Concepts by Ronda Heard

A WILEY PRESS BOOK
JOHN WILEY & SONS, INC.
New York • Chichester • Brisbane • Toronto • Singapore

Publisher: Judy V. Wilson
Editor: Alicia Conklin
Managing Editor: Maria Colligan
Illustrations drawn by Pat Collins
Composition and page make-up by Ganis and Harris, Inc.

Library of Congress Cataloging in Publication Data

Gault, Jan L.
Freetime: making your leisure count
    1. Leisure—Psychological aspects. 2. Success. I. Title.
GV14.4 G38   1983   790.01'32   82-24722

ISBN: 0-471-89041-3

Printed in the United States of America
83 84 10 9 8 7 6 5 4 3 2 1

This book is dedicated to my father,
Arthur Leon Vance
(November 17, 1907—September 23, 1973)
an entrepreneur, inventor, dreamer, nature lover, and free spirit

Contents

Acknowledgments

I would like to acknowledge my former students of psychology at Chaminade University in Honolulu for their patience, support, and suggestions while developing and testing some of the leisure questionnaires that have been adapted for this book. Also, those students of psychology and human development at the University of Hawaii for their time in responding to some of the leisure explorations.

Especially, I'd like to acknowledge my clients and seminar attendees in San Francisco, Marin, Berkeley, and throughout the world, without whom this book would not have been possible.

Finally, I want to thank my editor, Alicia Conklin, for her help and conscientious effort in guiding the manuscript toward its becoming a book.

Nothing should be prized more highly than the value of each day.

—Goethe

Introduction

In a sense, leisure touches on every aspect of life—our choices, our priorities, our goals, and ultimately our basic values. Leisure time is potentially available to more people today than ever before, yet most of us either aren't taking it or aren't using it very well.

In planning for a career, we carefully consider what we want and develop strategies for achieving our objectives. Our leisure time, however, is frequently up for grabs, according to chance, circumstance, or habit. We date and marry the people we just happen to bump into, whether they are the ones best suited to us or not. We get involved in activities and continue in pastimes that we derive little enjoyment or satisfaction from. We take vacations in spots totally unsuited to our personalities and needs. Demands, obligations, and interruptions bog us down so that we find it difficult to relax and have peace of mind even when we do have some spare time.

Most of all, we procrastinate. Tomorrow I'll begin dieting and stick with it; next week I'll stop smoking and get into a sound physical fitness program; and one of these days I'm going to set aside some time to put into action all the ideas I have on starting my own business, making my money grow, achieving more financial independence, and getting out of the 9-to-5 rut.

We believe that to achieve all these goals we must exert ourselves, push ourselves harder, put forth more effort, and muster up greater will power. But, in reality, we do not need to be superpeople to achieve our goals and do what we want to do. We do not even need to have any "will power." What we need is to stop making our lives so difficult. When there aren't any obstacles, we put some up. When, with a couple of easy maneuvers we could glide gently and surely toward our goals, we overlook the obvious route and stumble and struggle and lose our way.

So far as we know, we only have one life—one finite time frame that can be filled in a thousand different ways. Our slice of leisure is the free part of that time frame, the space where we have the possibility of choice, of transcending our circumstances and making decisions that will shape the content of life; to determine whether it will be filled with joy, love, riches, and beauty, or with boredom, worry, and frustration; whether it will be an adventurous challenge where success follows success, or a series of frustrating struggles that lead nowhere.

There are shortcuts that can save us time and ease us toward our goals. The sooner we know about them and put them into practice, the better. It is just as easy to set our goals high—and live well—as low, and far more pleasant.

The purpose of this book is to show you how to open up more free time without opening up Pandora's box. It will help you to take a fresh, clear look at that vast reservoir of leisure with its infinite possibilities, and show you how to use personal strategies to shape your leisure time to help you move gently and swiftly toward the peaks of success you desire.

I
THE LONG
PERSPECTIVE

Within the context of time, leisure is the free part of that space—the space where you have the possibility of choice. It is a time free from obligations, either to yourself or others, a time to do what you alone choose without feeling guilty about it or feeling that you ought to be doing something else. Leisure is the part of us that views life as an adventure; waking up in the morning and feeling good about the start of a new day. It is spontaneous laughter, learning, and loving, caring about ourself and others, the part of us that wants to dance and sing and skip about.

This, at least, is the potential of our leisure time. Yet most of us fail to use our leisure as creatively as we could. Rather than stimulating, refreshing, and revitalizing us, our leisure drains and enervates us. Why is this so? What is the nature of the dissatisfaction which plagues us? In the chapters that follow, we will examine these crucial questions.

1.
The Leisure Dilemma

He is never less at leisure than when at leisure.
—Cicero

What free time?

Today we find an increasing number of social scientists studying the "leisure problem"—that is, the use of all those extra hours that have evolved thanks to science and technology. Yet you wonder, "Where are they? Where do they go?" It seems as if we have more pressures, more demands on our time, more deadlines, endless stacks of paperwork, and we often feel just plain tired, frustrated, and overworked.

"What extra hours?" you ask. You spend two hours commuting to and from work, work overtime or maybe even hold a second part-time job to help keep up with inflation. Then there are all the requests for your time to help out at different civic and community groups. You want to do your share, but where does it all end? You would like to have more time to spend with your family, your friends, or even yourself. Shouldn't you have a little time left over just for you, to do what you alone want to do without feeling guilty about it?

Yet the potential for leisure has never been greater. With industrialization and automation, the average work week has decreased from 50, 60, or even 70 hours to the present average of below 40 hours. Many workers enjoy a four-day work week and flextime scheduling. Advances in medical science have increased the life span, and earlier retirement is possible through better pension programs.

Between 1900 and 1950, time after work doubled, and by the year 2000 it is expected to double again. Since 1940, we have had longer paid vacations and more holidays. The United States Department of Labor estimates that one fourth of the population is capable of producing all the goods and services for the rest of us.[1] No wonder leisure time is increasing!

1. *M. A. Holman, "A National Time-Budget for the Year 2000,"* Sociology and Social Research, *Vol. 46 (1961), pp. 17-25; P. Henle, "Recent Growth of Paid Leisure for U.S. Workers," in* Work and Leisure, *ed. E. O. Smigel (New Haven: College and University Press, 1963); Bureau of Labor Statistics, U.S. Department of Labor,* Employment and Earnings, *April, 1970.*

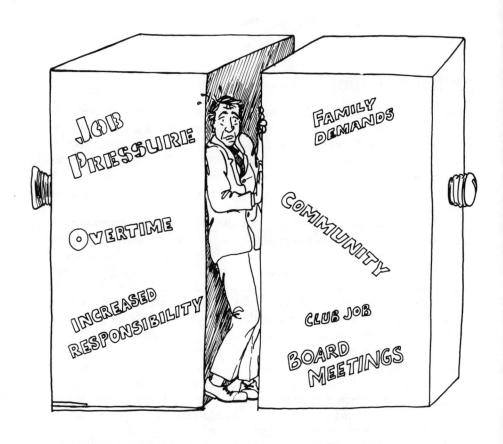

What leisure?

Without taking into account evening hours, a conservative schedule of weekends, holidays, and vacations gives us over *four months a year discretionary time*. Indeed, a society of part-time workers is likely in the not-too-distant future.

Potential leisure time = 4 months	
	DAYS OFF
HOLIDAYS	9
SATURDAYS	52
SUNDAYS	52
VACATIONS	10
TOTAL	123

What has happened to all this potential free time? The extra hours are there, but we never seem to have enough of them; we never "get caught up" with all we would like to do and accomplish. We feel *more* time pressure today, not less. Why is this so?

Back to the good old days

Sometimes, we dream about the "good old days" and wish we could go back in time to the simple life, away from the hectic rush of appointments, deadlines, regulations, schedules, and all the other headaches of modern living. We read the ads for acres of farmland in some remote spot and think about how blissful life must have been before modern civilization.

Regressing to earlier times, however, is unlikely to give us either the peace of mind or the life style we desire. Let's look at the past realistically. In prehistoric times, most people spent every moment in grubbing for a living, fighting off disease, and battling the harshest of weather conditions. A whole day might be spent in searching for a few edible roots to ward off starvation. Nights were spent in restless anxiety, alert to attacks by wild beasts or unfriendly tribes. No one had time to sit around and contemplate, "Who am I? Where am I going? What shall I do this weekend?" Only during a fleeting moment of wonder might a spark of awareness emerge. Life was harsh and death came early. Infant mortality rates were high. Female infanticide was a common practice among many tribes. Indeed, early death was a blessing for many. Life was "simple" only in the sense that all human energies were directed toward survival needs.

In earlier eras, no one had time to sit around and contemplate, "What shall I do this weekend?"

Only later in history did we discover how to have a measure of control. Control over the physical environment came first, as humans moved from a nomadic to an agricultural community. This dates back to the Neolithic revolution of the later part of the Stone Age. It occurred approximately 7000 years ago in Mesopotamia (an ancient country in Southwest Asia) and again, independently, 3000 years ago in Mesoamerica. With the domestication of plants and animals, people could stay in one place and reduce starvation. Nevertheless, a typical day still meant long hours of drudgery with little respite from the demands of survival. In most regions, work began at sunrise and did not cease until sunset. The working year was typically determined by the seasons; when the weather was good, work was hard; as inclement weather set in it slacked off. The periods of inactivity during the long, cold winter months were difficult. Famine and disease were widespread across the North Temperate Zone of the world. Time off from work was viewed with dread rather than anticipation.

Control over the social environment came later. As groups of people became settled into one place and their populations grew, some of the people were freed from the activity of food-getting. A division of labor was beginning to develop; supported by the farm community, some members of the villages could devote their time to religious, medical, or craft work. The majority, however, were still engaged in many hours of food production or other work vital to the maintenance and protection of the group.

With the Bronze Age, which began about 5000 years ago in the Middle East, the preindustrial city came into being. The division of labor became more extensive and systematic; castes, classes, and slavery were born. For the first time, a few of the people were freed from the need to spend all their hours working for a living. A small minority—an elite group—had emerged who did not have to work in order to survive. For the first time, for this small elite group, leisure became a reality.

However, accounts by historians or anthropologists of the existence of a few primitive tribes with leisurely life styles,[2] and of some ancient civilizations (notably those of Egypt, Babylonia, and Crete) with leisure classes, should not blind us to the fact that for the vast majority of people life throughout the ages has been a precarious struggle. Generally speaking, only a small number of elite societies in

---

2. *Turnbull, C.*, The Forest People *(New York: Simon and Schuster, Inc., 1962).*

earlier eras have known leisure, and then only by virtue of the toil of subjugated populations. Even during the Classical Age of Greece there were four slaves for every free Athenian man.

It was not until the Renaissance that the foundation was laid for the formulation of a truly egalitarian leisure society. Today, with continued advances in science and technology, we can envision the possibility of meeting every person's primary needs and expanding leisure time beyond special groups. We can visualize free time, extra hours, not only for an elite group supported by serfs or slaves, but for each person.

Most people who have tried to turn back time and return to a simpler existence have soon become disillusioned. Several years ago, an article in the *Wall Street Journal* told how many financially successful corporate executives were dropping out and leaving the rat race to explore the "simpler" life. They headed for the farms, the woods, and the rural communities in an effort to get away from it all and have more leisure and peace of mind. However, as the days grew longer and the hours stretched out in front of them, they soon began taking on whatever nonpressure, makeshift jobs were available as clerks, service station attendants, or carpenters. A follow-up study of these same men later showed that most of them had quickly become disenchanted and bored. After a short period, they were returning to the cities and to their old jobs. Although neither alternative was fully satisfactory, other options were not explored.

The discomfort of leisure

One of humanity's major goals has been the conservation of time, yet, paradoxically, the *more* free time we have, the *less* is our life satisfaction.[3] As more time becomes available, we soon begin to feel anxious and scramble to fill up the hours, often getting ourselves locked into stress-producing situations. Today, although we have the possibility of more leisure time and a more rewarding life style than ever before, we find dissatisfaction and stress rampant.

Among my clients and students in my work as a leisure management consultant, I have found the leisure dilemma to center on two extreme personalities. On the one hand, there are the workaholics, who never find enough free time. They may work six or seven days a week, with evenings spent in work or work-related activities. The

---

3. *"Time: A Measure of our Values,"* The Futurist, *June, 1980, pp. 201-202.*

The minutes and hours slip away

workaholic may be a corporate executive, an attorney, a physician, a systems analyst, an accountant, a professor, a sales representative, a student, a housewife, or what have you. Yet all suffer from a sense of pressure and urgency to get things done, as if driven by a never-ending series of "must-do's" and "should-do's." The workaholic feels little sense of choice or freedom. There is *always* something that needs to be done.

At the other extreme are those few persons who confess to having too much time on their hands, such as the retired or nonemployed. In contrast to the workaholic, the person with a surplus of leisure is more likely to express discontentment and to feel bored or apathetic. With the workaholic, only a nagging feeling now and then creeps in, suggesting that maybe "something" is missing from his or her life.

Here are some typical complaints about leisure that I hear from clients:

"I often feel a lot of pressure to do things I do not want to do or enjoy doing."

"When I do have some free time, I have difficulty relaxing and letting go of the demands and obligations of the day."

"I sometimes feel discouraged and a lack of accomplishment. I know I could be doing more, but I cannot seem to get the important things in my life done."

"I procrastinate all too frequently, putting off what I need to be doing, and then I feel awful about it, as the minutes and hours slip away."

"It seems like I'm spending a lot of money on entertainment . . . and not having all that much fun or getting that much out of it."

"I would like to realize more zest from life."

Most of my clients and students are not maladjusted or drastically unhappy with their lives. If I were to ask any one of them, "How are you doing?" I'd probably get a response something like, "Okay," "So-so," "Not that bad," "Fine most of the time." They are, in general, reasonably happy, well-adjusted, intelligent people who from time to time simply feel a certain uneasiness or a sense that things could perhaps be better—maybe a lot better.

As I probe further, however, I find that there are a wide range of differences and degrees of satisfaction. One person's entire social life may consist of a Friday night movie with a friend. Another will tell me how important physical fitness is to him, but finds that walking a short distance to the bus every morning is all the activity he has been able to muster in the last few years.

Marlene, a bright woman in her mid-thirties, told me on one of her

Time on our hands

first visits to my office how much she enjoyed playing the piano, but she hadn't taken the time to play for *over twelve years*. Donna, an attractive brunette, told me that she loved to go to parties and meet people but had gotten into the habit of spending most of her time at home reading novels and dreaming of what might be.

Inconsistencies between what we do and what we would like to do are all too common and can sometimes end in a vicious cycle. Mark, a middle-aged corporate attorney, explained to me how much he would like to spend more time at home with his family, but long hours at work and late meetings always seemed to preclude time at home. As a result, his wife had started feeling neglected and began complaining even when he was around. Their sex life soon dropped to practically nil, with Mark feeling frustrated and guilty. After a while, even when he was able to finish work early, he found himself spending more time away from home at the neighborhood bar. Variations on this theme are repeated over and over in our society today.

Joyce, a recent divorcée, would like to meet some interesting men, but comes home from work feeling tired and listless. She eats dinner alone in front of the television set, wishing someone would call her.

John retired from the military at the age of forty-three. He drives a taxi now because, in his words, "I have to do something with my time."

Gina finds that when she's feeling down, buying a new pair of shoes, some perfume, or a new dress fills up the time better than sitting home doing nothing, and for a while she forgets her depression.

Bill, a handsome young bachelor, quit work three years ago on inheriting a small fortune, and spent his time traveling from one country to another. When he came in to see me he had lost all desire for further travel and wasn't sure what he wanted to do.

Each of these people has found a means of coping with his or her leisure time, whether it be burying themselves in their work, over-extending themselves in after-work obligations, going on shopping sprees, daydreaming, traveling aimlessly, or letting the television fill up their hours.

We value time and seek to conserve this valuable resource, yet find time on our hands a burden too heavy to bear. We demand more freedom to choose, yet the moment we are handed a block of time to use in whatever way we wish, we become upset, suffer from the burden of over-choice, the guilt of not doing the "right" thing, the fear of being selfish, hedonistic, or egotistical, the blame of indulging ourselves, and the final anguish of wasting our gift of time without finding any real source of meaning, joy, or love.

The weight of others' demands can keep you feeling bogged down

Common leisure ailments

In spite of the potential for leisure in our lives today, most of us find our time space filled with anything but leisure. Procrastination, worry, apathy, pressure, and demands take over our time and diminish our zest for living. Although the dissatisfactions with leisure life styles vary from individual to individual, several common leisure ailments can be identified.

External pressures: "Everyone's pressuring me!"

Whether you are self-employed, an executive, a housewife, a student, or between jobs, the weight of others' demands can keep you feeling bogged down and lacking control over your own life. Does one of the following situations sound familiar?

- Your employer gives you an urgent assignment, and then thoughtlessly interrupts you with so many other tasks that you find yourself working late into the night to meet your deadline.
- You believe you're doing a knockout job as coordinator of this year's fund-raising event for your charity or civic organization, but everyone else seems to have their own ideas about how it could be done better.
- No matter what you do for your mate, it never seems to be quite enough. Your mate doesn't come right out and express his or her displeasure, but it hangs in the air between you like thick smog, stifling further communication.
- You're all too aware that you are not spending enough time with your children. You are long overdue on letters to good friends. The garage still needs to be cleaned out. And you really should go to that seminar next weekend that your boss recommended.

These are typical symptoms of one of the most common leisure ailments: an inability to escape from the demands placed on you by others, which makes it impossible to find time for the activities that would be most rewarding, stimulating, and creative *for you.*

Vacation woes: "All that money, and everything went wrong!"

A vacation today may cost you anywhere from $500 to $5,000. But how many people return home from their vacations feeling refreshed and stimulated? Most people return home enervated by the amazing

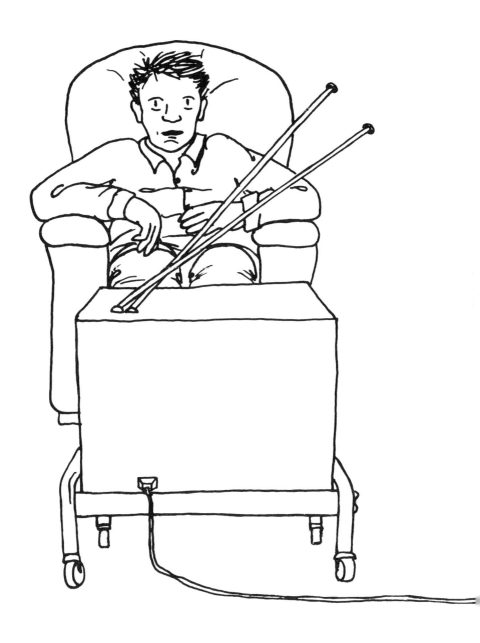

Killing time

number of things that went wrong, ready to go back to work and get into a regular routine again. The best part of many vacations turns out to be the preparation and happy anticipation *before* the trip.

You can probably remember going to a vacation spot that was highly recommended only to find that it was definitely not your "place in the sun." Before the trip, it sounded exciting to travel thousands of miles across the ocean to some foreign land. Sleek travel brochures stimulate your fantasies, and you are keyed up for new romance, fine dining, and exotic sights. But your overly romantic expectations are often dashed by the dispiriting reality: dysentery, high prices, and hot, jammed tour buses turn out to be the order of the day.

A common leisure ailment is choosing a vacation spot that doesn't suit your needs, interests, or tastes. A lover of the big city and of all the modern conveniences, you may decide one year to be a sport and go along with your spouse's wish to go camping in a remote region of Australia. Thrilled, he plunks down $3,600 for the airfare and a month's reservation at a campsite near Latora, miles off the beaten track. After the fourth day of cooking and cleaning up, fighting off strange crawling creatures, mosquitos, and tossing in a rock-hard sleeping bag all night, your irritation explodes, and the vacation becomes a disaster for everyone.

Wasting your precious vacation time and money on an inappropriate, unsatisfying trip is our second common leisure ailment.

Killing time: "I don't know where the time goes."

Many of our waking hours are spent in killing time. We kill time waiting in lines at the doctor's or dentist's office, at the grocery checkout counter, at the service station, and at the bank. We wait for buses, trains, and airplanes. We wait for business meetings and dates with friends. It may be for only a few minutes, or for a half hour or longer. Either way, this idle time is *dead time.*

You may find that you have a bit of time here and a bit of time there, but never quite enough to allow you to get into the priority tasks in your life. Over the years, these spare minutes and hours add up to an enormous amount of dead time. By the age of forty, you may have wasted more than *eight years* just sitting around doing nothing.[4] These idle hours are a deadly—and all too common—leisure ailment.

----

4. *"Do You Waste Your Spare Time?"* San Francisco Chronicle, *September 21, 1981, p. 31.*

Locked into relationships

Unfulfilling relationships: "My social life could be better."

Many of us find ourselves locked into personal relationships that we do not especially enjoy or value but continue out of lethargy, habit, or fear. Instead of making the effort to meet new people, we fall back on old relationships and friendships that we have long outgrown or that were never particularly satisfying.

Sometimes we simply do not want to be alone, and so we pick up the telephone to talk with someone—anyone. Or we make plans to be with someone on Saturday evening not because we really want to be with him or her but to avoid the unpleasant prospect of sitting home alone. "I should be out having fun on a Saturday night," we tell ourselves. Sitting home alone with six hours of time on our hands is an uncomfortable thought. The inability to break out of this kind of routine, unsatisfying relationship is a fourth common leisure ailment.

Spending sprees: "I never seem to get out of debt."

Americans spend over $218 billion a year on leisure,[5] yet there may be no relationship between the dollars spent and the personal satisfaction obtained. You buy a boat that goes to sea a few times, then stays put forever in its slip at shore. Going diving in scuba gear sounded like fun from the advertisements, but one time out was enough, and now the expensive gear remains somewhere in the back of a closet. You hope to inspire your talented child and buy her one of the best violins. She loses interest in the instrument after three months.

If much of your spending consists of shopping sprees motivated by boredom, a need to fill the void in your leisure time, or the commercial pressures all around us in today's society, you are a victim of the fifth common leisure ailment.

Procrastination: "I know I can do it, but the time just isn't right yet."

If you have never clearly identified the value of leisure in your life, or chosen a direction for your leisure which might enhance your well-being, when you do have some time left over for yourself, you may feel

---

5. *"Americans Play Even With Economy in Spin,"* U.S. News and World Report, *September 8, 1980, p. 52.*

Trying to climb out of debt

listless, discouraged, and frustrated. There is so much I could do, you tell yourself, if only I could get started and stay with it. Yet for many people, starting and pursuing a project, even an enjoyable and rewarding one, is very difficult. We daydream about completing the artwork we began and abandoned long ago, about finishing that half-finished book, or even about just getting our files in order. And as the hours, days, months, and years slip away, the more difficult and intimidating the tasks seem to become. These are the symptoms of procrastination, the sixth common leisure ailment.

What's the reason for our malaise?

Where do these leisure ailments come from? Why do they persist? The answers to these questions are to be found in our *attitudes* toward leisure and in our education, that, for the most part, fails to address the creative use of leisure. The answers also involve the myths and false expectations that we have concerning work and our careers, and our failure to identify the rich potential of leisure in our lives today. We will look at each of these factors more closely in the following chapters.

How does your leisure life style rate?

Before you go on to the next chapter, take the short quiz below. It is designed to tell you how effectively you are presently using your leisure time. Score each of the following statements from one to five, according to this key:

1   Almost never
2   Rarely
3   Occasionally
4   Fairly often
5   Almost always

Statements   **Your score**

I thoroughly enjoy my leisure time.   4

My spare time is free of pressures, obligations, and demands.   4

My social needs are being satisfactorily met in my leisure hours.   3

I have a creative outlet that I pursue during my free time.   _5_

My leisure life style promotes good health and physical fitness.   _2_

I value the minutes of my spare time and do not procrastinate or just kill time.   _2_

My use of leisure contributes to my emotional well-being.   _3_

I plan my spare time in accordance with the priority of my leisure goals.   _2_

My leisure activities contribute to or improve my personal relationships.   _3_

I use my leisure time to discover and fulfill my talents and abilities.   _3_

My leisure activities meet important personal needs that are not being met at work.   _5_

Overall, my leisure activities have a positive effect upon my life.   _3_

Add up your points and check your leisure lifestyle according to the scale below:

55-60   You have established sound leisure habits and are effectively using your leisure time. Your leisure activities are consistent with your desires, ambitions, and values. Your choice of leisure pastimes is dictated by what you want to do rather than what others try to pressure you into doing. You have probably thought about the benefits of leisure for your life and are following through for good physical/mental well-being and personal success.

47-54   You are moderately effective in using your leisure time. In general, your leisure activities contribute to your personal growth, fitness, social needs, and success. Although you are not always making the most of your leisure, you do not waste a lot of time and tend to enjoy yourself.

34-46   Things are going all right for you during your leisure hours, but they could be much better. Sometimes you participate in activities that enhance your personal development, fitness, relationships, and well-being. Frequently, however, it's hit-

and-miss. You may find yourself responding to the pressures and demands of others, and not having enough time for yourself. You are likely to procrastinate, and are not using your creative talents and abilities as well as you might.

24-33 There is a strong need for improvement in your use of leisure time. Your personal and social needs are being only minimally met during your free time. For the most part, you are not enjoying and benefiting from your leisure.

23 and It does not appear that your time is important to you. Perhaps **below** you have not thought through the value of leisure for your life, and the ways in which it can promote your success and well-being.

These scores represent one way to rate your leisure life style. If you did not score as high as you would have liked, do not despair. In later chapters a number of self-explorations will help you to identify exactly what factors might be intruding on your leisure time, and what you can do to make your leisure and your life more rewarding.

2.
How Your Attitudes Toward Leisure Affect You

A life of leisure and a life of laziness are two things.
—Benjamin Franklin

Attitudes toward leisure have changed dramatically during the course of history. Formerly leisure was viewed as an end in itself and a prized ideal toward which to strive; today in Western society it is associated with hedonism, laziness, and sin. Understanding this historical change can help us to understand and control our own attitudes and, ultimately, our lives.

Leisure as time for learning and understanding

The ancient Greeks are credited with discovering leisure,[1] and the Greek philosophers of about 500 B.C. to 300 B.C. formulated a positive leisure ideal. Leisure was valued, and work was not seen as central to life. Indeed, work was viewed as a curse and an enemy of the free man. As Aristotle expressed it in the *Nicomachean Ethics*, a person's true life was not to be found in work but in leisure. Work was seen as instrumental to the goal of a life of leisure. For Aristotle, leisure represented the person's highest goal, the possibility of the achievement of understanding.

Our concept of leisure comes from the Greek notion of *scholē*, related to our word *school*. It formerly meant a time of peace and quiet but later came to mean having time to oneself for contemplation. Aristotle believed that through contemplation you would dis-

---

1. deGrazia, S., Of Time, Work and Leisure *(New York: Anchor Books, 1960).*

cover truth and know beauty. Labor was seen as an activity that distracted from one's pursuit of knowledge and understanding, and was therefore to be avoided.

Plato maintained that in moving toward your own self-perfection by devoting time to thinking, learning, play, and self-expression, you would discover true happiness. This, to Plato, was leisure. For Aristotle, free time per se was not leisure, but *free time used wisely*. This meant cultivation of the mind through music and study as well as keeping physically fit by participation in sports.

Unlike in modern Western societies, the quality of life and happiness for the Greeks depended solely on one's leisure life rather than one's work. Early education in leisure skills was an important socialization process of the Greeks. It was leisure that formed the basis for the development of a person's self-concept and life satisfaction.

Leisure as hedonistic pleasure

The early Romans also held positive attitudes toward leisure in some ways similar to those of the Greeks. Like the Greeks, the Romans were interested in sports and the theater. And in the first stages of the Roman Empire, there was much active participation in sports and games, especially as a means of keeping fit and being able to fight for the state. Unlike among the Greeks, leisure was not seen as an ultimate goal or valued for its own sake.

While the Greeks stressed learning and self-fulfillment as the essential leisure ideal, the Romans' time became taken up more and more with spectator activities, hedonistic pleasures, and diversions. They are well known for their hundreds of public baths, their circuses for chariot racing, and their gladiatorial combats. Diversions and pleasure-seeking forms of entertainment were especially popular in the latter days of the empire. Social entertainment reached its peak in A.D. 354, when the Roman year included 200 public holidays. The downfall of Rome may well be attributed to the people's inability to use their leisure wisely.

Leisure as restoration for work

After the fall of the Roman Empire, a reaction to the idleness and pleasure-seeking of the Romans developed. The conquerors condemned the Roman way of life, and stressed the virtue of hard work.

Throughout the Middle Ages for the next millennium, long hours of physical labor and harsh conditions were the way of life of most people. The little leisure available was regarded as a time for recuperation, relaxation, and restoration for another day of work.

A rigid social structure existed during this period, and the amount of free time was strictly determined by one's social class. The four main classes were the clergy, the lords and knights, the merchants, and the peasants, with peasants making up the greatest part of the population. Dancing, singing, and games of chance were popular pastimes when some time existed. Although religious holidays abounded in the medieval period, they were filled with religious rituals and obligations, and had little resemblance to holidays as we know them in the twentieth century.

Philosophers such as St. Augustine and St. Thomas Aquinas expressed the changing attitudes toward work found during this period. Work began to be thought of not just as a duty and drudgery, but as having dignity and meaning in its own right. Any idle time took on a negative connotation. The writings of the medieval philosophers reflect the emerging attitudes of Western civilization toward work and leisure. Although the work ethic is usually considered to have its origin with the Reformation in the seventeenth century, at least one social scientist, Richard Kraus, sees the work ethic as dating back to the medieval period.[2]

Leisure as laziness and sin

As the Middle Ages drew to a close, several forces had an impact on attitudes toward work and leisure. With the Renaissance there was a reawakening in science, philosophy, and the arts. The static social structure of the medieval period began to break down, and more people in the cities of Europe were able to gain upward mobility. Through individual effort and work they were now able to enhance their positions. The Reformation, and especially the doctrines of Calvinism, furthered a work orientation and negative feelings toward any leisure. Calvinism implied that man through his works and a frugal, ascetic life style would be able to gain salvation. Belief in these doctrines apparently was one of the strong motivating forces that led men to work hard and deny themselves pleasures.

---

2. *R. Kraus,* Recreation and Leisure in Modern Society *(New York: Appleton Century Crofts, 1971).*

An austere Puritan ethic developed, and in some areas gambling, dancing, gay singing, festivals, and other pleasures were banned. Leisure activity was referred to as "the beginning of evil" and "the end goal on which all sins are honored." This Puritan work ethic was felt all across Northwestern Europe and North America, especially in New England.

Although the seventeenth and eighteenth century philosophers Locke and Rousseau believed in the value of play, games, and sports, they saw these activities primarily as serving utilitarian purposes—to strengthen one's character, prevent idleness, and curb antisocial behavior.

In America, a strong work orientation was probably related not only to the Puritan Protestantism that was so influential in the seventeenth century, but also to the natural environmental conditions that required hard work of the early colonists and pioneers. Another factor was the increasing upward mobility that occurred

Leisure—the beginning of evil?

among the middle classes in America as an apparent result of their individual work efforts.

These attitudes toward work and leisure are still very much a part of our life today. Leisure is often seen as synonymous with idleness, a period where the person's natural laziness is cultivated and coddled. The saying, "Idleness is the devil's keeper" expresses this sentiment. Values built into Western culture tend to associate honesty and hard work with success, while leisure and laziness are linked together.

The stigma of leisure

Ask someone about their leisure time and, regardless of how much free time may be potentially available to them, they are likely to respond, "*What* leisure?" No one, it seems, likes to admit to having leisure time. It carries a stigma, as if leisure were morally wrong. We like to think of ourselves as always busy, active, and on the move. Frequently when a prospective client telephones me to ask about my program in leisure, he or she will justify the inquiry with comments such as, "The only reason I'm calling is that right now I'm in between jobs," or "I've just recently been divorced and I feel a void in my life." They feel a need to excuse themselves for having some free time or for being dissatisfied with their use of that time. We feel so guilty about any excess of time that even thinking about how we might increase this precious commodity apparently generates remorse. Only during midlife and the sudden realization that hard work and honesty alone have not resulted in the kinds of successes we had hoped to achieve, do many people begin to question the Puritan work ethic.

Although writers today speak of the decline of the work ethic, I find it to still be prevalent for the majority of people. Once I was conferring with a division of the federal government about offering a leisure education program for their employees. The government officials were worried about what the taxpayers' attitude might be toward such a program. Education in leisure? Isn't that a waste of time and money? But, as we shall see, leisure is not merely the opposite of work. Rather, as one writer puts it, "it is the opportunity for free participation in the joyful activity and rest of those who are exploring the full potential of creation."[3] Considered in this way, the fullest use of leisure is no waste of time or money; on the contrary, it is an investment in the creativity of human beings.

---

3. quotation by *Colin Wilbur Williams*.

Lack of a leisure identity

We are still in the Dark Ages when it comes to our leisure life style. Our educational institutions attempt to prepare us for a career, yet they show little awareness of the benefits of leisure for our lives. Ever since we were kids, we have been taught the importance of career goals. "What are you going to be when you grow up? Doctor, fireman, teacher, actor . . ." Who ever asked, "What kind of *person* would you like to be when you grow up—empathic, loving, cooperative?" The emphasis is always on a *job*—that narrow area of life that is shrinking daily.

So even though our work today accounts for less than one third of our time, our identity is still largely tied up with our jobs and careers. We continue to think of ourselves as white-collar workers, blue-collar workers, staff or line employees, professionals, corporate executives, unemployed, or retired. We approach the loss of a job or the prospect of retirement with anxiety. And this is generally true regardless of our financial situation. How many people have "retired" only to go back to work again after a few months? Being without work makes many people fearful.

What is the basis of these fears? Why do we feel useless, unwanted, and worthless when we cannot define ourselves through an occupation?

Realistically, what do we face without a job? A lack of self-worth because we are not being paid for our services? But what is the relationship between what you are paid and your value as a person? Does the minimum wage truly express the value of your life? Does $10.00 an hour, or $100.00 an hour? Boxers, entertainers, and football pros can earn hundreds of thousands or millions of dollars per year, while university presidents and distinguished professors earn less than $60,000 annually. We can all think of occupational comparisons that are inconsistent in terms of dollars received and value. Nevertheless, our self-esteem is often related to our earning power in the work setting. But can we in fact put a true value on a person's life according to *any* monetary compensation received? The answer, it seems to me, is clearly no.

Meaning in work or leisure?

We take for granted that work is central to our lives. We look to work for self-fulfillment, stimulation and interest. But how many of us find

Self-fulfillment in work or leisure?

that much meaning in our work? How many of us wake up dreading the 9-to-5 grind?

Even in the best of jobs, much work is tedious, routine, and boring. One of my clients, who heads a large corporation, once told me that he found his job stimulating and challenging, yet in keeping a log and recording his reactions to daily tasks, he discovered that *less than 15 percent* of his responsibilities were challenging or provided any opportunities for creativity. (You'll learn how to keep such a log, and how to use it to improve your use of time, a little later in this book.)

Another client of mine, an experienced high-school math teacher who is knowledgeable, dedicated, and a fine instructor, estimated that with time for testing, grading papers, keeping discipline, and attending meetings, barely 20 percent of her time was spent in communicating ideas and stimulating curiosity and interest in the classroom.

Even a physician confessed to me that the bulk of his duties were perfunctory and boring. Whether you are a business executive, a consultant, a teacher, an attorney or what-have-you, it is likely that big chunks of your time are taken up with paperwork, unpleasant meetings, or other work that provides minimal opportunities for creativity and personal fulfillment.

How much more potential we have for stimulation, creativity, and personal development in our leisure hours! Yet for many of us, the prospect of a long stretch of leisure time is about as pleasant as the thought of serving a term in prison. What will we do, we ask? We can only travel or play tennis so long before apathy and fatigue set in. We do not know how to plan our leisure time effectively.

Lack of leisure planning

The idea of leisure planning is an unfamiliar one. In our leisure hours, we expect wonderful things to simply happen: fun, excitement, great relationships, interesting social activities—all with little or no effort on our part. But nothing much is very likely to happen in our leisure time unless we make it happen.

Leisure planning means taking a look at the whole realm of leisure-time possibilities—from remodeling your home, gardening, or creating a work of art, to learning more about yourself and the world in which you live. It means taking a look at the many possibilities, learning how they relate to your values and interests, and how they might meet your goals and priorities.

We often see goals as confined to our career interests. But without a clear idea of our leisure-time goals, we tend to drift in and out of a series of unrelated activities, spend too much time as passive spectators and become prone to others' influence and pressure in what should be our free time.

To get out of this rut, it's necessary first to recognize your own potential for creative and fulfilling leisure.

3.
Your Leisure
Potential

He hath no leisure who useth it not.
—George Herbert

Each of us has an enormous unrealized potential. Your brain weighs a mere three pounds and accounts for less than two percent of your total weight, yet it contains over twelve billion neurons (nerve cells), each with a potential for thought and creativity. If every atom in your brain were the size of a one-carat diamond, these atoms would fill up the entire forty-eight floors of the San Francisco pyramid building— and then some. Yet most people have tapped no more than ten percent of this potential. It's like having a giant computer at your disposal without having told the operator how to use it.

Part of the explanation for this dormancy lies in our present stage of development. In our individual history and in our self-understanding, we are still infants, barely becoming aware of ourselves and all our mind resources. We have known ourselves but a short time, are in fact just beginning to get to know ourselves. In spite of all our impressive technological accomplishments, our "self" is a new emergent in history, barely cognizant, and, even today, at a very rudimentary level of awareness and organization. We are just beginning to discover how you can consciously shape this great potential within yourself.

In the past, our beliefs and behaviors have for the most part been dictated by chance and circumstance. From the day you were born you have been getting input from the world: some good, some bad; some true, some false. Throughout the socialization process, information has flowed in from parents, teachers, siblings, peers, and the communications media of society. All this has been programmed in for better or for worse. And you have done the best you can, trying to sort it out, make some sense of the jungle of information out there, and grope your way along in an irrational world.

We are fond of saying that we learn from experience, and to a certain extent we do, but we also need to remind ourselves that experience teaches lies. Our input is made up not only of facts, but also of half-truths, distorted truths, biases, and prejudices. It is neither completely logical, systematic, nor coherent. And no one out there is necessarily giving us the input that is most accurate or best for us at any time.

The beliefs, opinions, biases, and motivations that constitute the self have been shaped by all sorts of factors outside of your control: how often we hear something repeated, who says it, how they say it, when they say it, the clothes they are wearing, their demeanor, your attention and mood at the moment, and so on. In short, dozens of irrelevant factors which may have no bearing on the accuracy or truth of what you are picking up and being "programmed" with go into what you are today. It is out of this whole body of past experience that you think, feel, and act.

Most of us like to view ourselves as men and women of action who make our own decisions and control our own destinies. And we all do in limited ways. The aim here is to provide you with the means to dislodge and release the past time mold of any inaccuracies and irrationalities that are contracting your leisure potential and preventing you from getting the results you want. That may be to experience greater freedom, become more creative, have better health, reduce excesses, or feel younger, more alive and energetic. In other words, instead of just letting things happen to you, hit-or-miss, sometimes good, sometimes bad, we now have the means whereby you can begin to take charge and create a time space of your own choosing and design.

Leisure: the elusive concept

Traditionally, leisure is thought of as time left over after work, i.e., the activities for which you are paid. But another way to think about leisure—and perhaps a more constructive way—is as a state of mind, as a raw commodity or a potential to be shaped and molded into whatever you desire; as a time in which your individual personality can find its true expression.

According to this more subjective interpretation, leisure is a time to *be*, to *know*, to *experience*, and to *do* everything you dream of; to make those choices most compatible with your needs and desires; to be productive, to create, to learn, to understand, to laugh, to be inspired, or just to play. Max Kaplan, a leading sociologist in the field of leisure, has suggested that in our leisure we stand exposed because leisure is that time when we are freest to be ourselves. Therefore, what we do in our leisure is an indication of *what* we are, *who* we are, and the *direction* in which we're headed:[1]

Carving out the time space of your choice

Leisure and success

Leisure and success are a two-way street. As you become more successful, you have the possibility of increasing your amount of leisure, and with more leisure, your opportunities for greater success

1. M. Kaplan, Leisure in America: A Social Inquiry (New York: John Wiley & Sons, 1960), pp. 4-5.

mushroom. Achieving success through leisure means taking charge of your life to create the kinds of success you desire, whether it be personal, social, or financial.

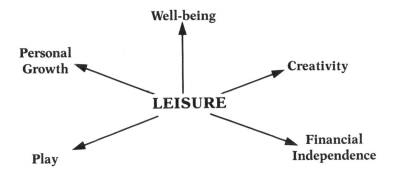

Leisure and success are a two-way street

LEISURE

In today's volatile economic and political climate, achieving financial success solely through a job is extremely difficult. You can no longer work at a job and confidently tuck your earnings away in a bank, in blue chip stocks, or in bonds and expect to come out ahead or even stay afloat. Most people today have more difficulty in taking care of their money than in making it.

It is not unusual for one of my clients to complain that he or she is working seventy-plus hours per week—perhaps even holding two jobs—and is still barely managing to break even, regardless of earnings. For such people, establishing more of a balance between work and leisure generally produces several positive results. By taking time for a regular exercise program and paying more attention to their physical and psychological well-being, they become more alert and creative when they are at work, do a better job, and are more likely to be promoted and receive salary increases. And by setting aside some of their spare time to adequately consider their investment objectives and strategies, they find themselves enjoying a higher rate of return on their money.

Establishing sound leisure habits can net work
promotions and extra dollars

Robert, a sales executive for a large computer firm, found that by eliminating evening overtime hours and spending more time jogging, he became more alert on the job and netted two promotions and salary increases within only six months. Tom, an overworked and financially strapped corporate attorney, cut out weekend overtime and devoted some of that time to locating sound real estate investments. In less than three years he was able to triple his assets, and felt much better physically as well.

Nora, a psychology counselor with good business aptitude, started taking some spare time to read a few select financial newsletters and discovered that she could really make money in the stock market, a hobby she had previously toyed with for years with little success.

Only by setting aside some spare time to invest in your physical and psychological health and to better educate yourself as a wiser investor and consumer are you likely to stretch out your dollars, conquer inflation, and accumulate a measure of wealth.

Leisure can have other benefits as well. Your potential for creativity and personal development in your leisure hours is virtually unlimited. Throughout history, major contributions to science, the arts, and human welfare have been made by people outside of the work setting during their leisure hours. Leonardo da Vinci and Benjamin Franklin are famous examples of men who achieved much outside of their everyday work. Geoffrey Chaucer, one of the world's greatest poets, earned his living as a customs collector.

Major breakthroughs in the science of genetics were made by Gregor Mendel, the abbot of a monastery. Anton Van Leeuwenhoek, a dry-goods merchant, is known for his discoveries in microbiology. Jean Henri Fabre, a teacher of the classics, made contributions in zoology. Nathaniel Hawthorne had a routine job working at a customs house, yet he managed to produce four novels, including the classic *The Scarlet Letter*, in his spare time. Some of our most noted novelists have been practicing physicians.

One of the key elements in these leisure-time achievements was a sense of freedom and playfulness. Being able to "play around" with ideas, words, or symbols while free from pressures and time constraints can open the door to innovation and creativity. Another factor was the sense of purpose and commitment these people brought to their leisure. Each took a block of time and shaped it into a work of art, a dream, or a tangible creation.

In his classic work *The Achieving Society*, David McClelland noted that, historically, peaks of leisure have coincided with peaks of cultural growth. During periods of abundant leisure, the arts and

By setting aside some of our spare time to educate
ourselves as wiser investors and consumers, we
can stretch our dollars

sciences have flourished and humanity has moved away from ignorance and superstition and toward more humane forms of relationships.[2] The promise of peace in the world today may well be determined by our leisure choices.

While you may not aspire to be a great scientist, artist, or poet, it is during your leisure hours—that time when you are freest to be yourself—that you can achieve those personal successes that are most consistent with your values and interests.

2. D. C. McClelland, The Achieving Society (Princeton: D. Van Nostrand, 1961).

II
HOW YOU USE
YOUR LEISURE
NOW

You are piloting a one-engine Cessna 152 airplane and have been hit by a bitter snowstorm. The radio is out, and you are hopelessly lost. Low on fuel and losing power, you are forced into an emergency landing. Safely on the ground, you look around in an attempt to get your bearings. Although you are stocked with dozens of maps and charts, you find yourself floundering, unsure of which direction to take. Perhaps you will get lucky and someone will come to your rescue. Or you may happen onto some familiar landmark and find your way before fatigue and hunger end your search. Without knowing where you are, however, the odds of getting somewhere in the shortest possible time are remote.

The first step in realizing the many rewards possible from leisure is figuring out where you are now in your use of leisure time. Until you do, all the maps and guides in the world will not help you to get to where you want to go.

To figure this out, you will need to answer questions like these: What activities are you participating in during your spare time? What are you getting out of them? How much time are you spending on those things that are most important to you? How much time do you spend with the people you truly care about, and what is the quality of that time? What proportion of your time have you set aside just for you—to do what you genuinely enjoy doing—without feeling apologetic or having misgivings? How does your leisure compensate for any shortcomings in your job situation? What myths and misconceptions about work, leisure, and change are restricting your freedom and joy in living? How do time—and energy—consuming emotional downs or conflicts prevent you from achieving your goals?

To help you assess your current use of leisure time and to pinpoint your areas of satisfaction and dissatisfaction, in the following two chapters we will: (1) Examine a number of myths and false notions about work, leisure, and change that may be limiting your capacity for greater success; and (2) Engage in a series of explorations to clarify your leisure interests, patterns, and motivations.

The final chapters will then provide you with a plan of action for bridging the gap between your present use of leisure time and the use that could maximize your personal successes.

4.
Myths That Hold You Back

The end of labor is to gain leisure.

—Aristotle

Myths about work and leisure

Myth #1: Idle hands are the devil's keeper.

When we have time on our hands, we often feel guilty or anxious. As we noted in Chapter Two, this goes back to the Puritan work ethic, which equates hard work with success. But some of the most successful, creative, and happy people are not those who work the hardest but those who know how to organize their work time to leave time for those things that are important to them—having improved relationships, developing a new interest or hobby, commiting themselves to a social cause, or just spending some time basking in the sun.

In trying to beat the clock in pursuit of our career goals, we fail to examine our whole-life priorities. Viewed from the perspective of the total scheme of things, what is the rush? Where do we think we are going? An abundance of studies show that many persons who push themselves relentlessly are indeed headed for illness, ulcers, and heart attacks.[1]

The individuals today who will no doubt give us our greatest insights and contribute the most to the quality of human life are those who have learned how to relax, to play, and to love, and have not lost the sense of awe, wonder, and beauty to be found only when one is truly at leisure.

---

1. *M. Friedman and R. H. Rosenman,* Type A. Behavior and your Heart *(New York: Random House, 1974);* N. Howard and S. Antilla, *"Thank god it's Monday,"* Dun's Review, *June 1981, pp. 46-50.*

With too much time on my hands, I feel anxious

Myth #2: We find meaning through work rather than leisure.

For decades, society has been concerned with the search for meaning and self-fulfillment in the work setting. With the advent of automation, a deluge of literature examined the problems of the alienated worker and the undermining effects of a loss of meaning in work. Today firms are paying management consultants hundreds of thousands of dollars to tell them how they can make work more meaningful for their employees. It is commonly believed that if work is more self-fulfilling, employees will be better motivated and there will be reduced tardiness, absenteeism, and turnover.

More realistically, however, what is needed is that the employees' expectations be set straight. As we have seen, even in the best of jobs, a big chunk of time is spent on details and distasteful duties. Furthermore, our hours at work account for less than one third of our total time and continue to shrink. Far better to look to leisure rather than work for personal fulfillment, creative outlets, and more meaning in life.

Myth #3: Leisure requires no planning or commitment.

If we think about leisure at all, we tend to think about it as something that just happens and requires little consideration on our part. And if leisure were only a period of recovery from work, this might be true. But most of us do not require the eight or more hours we have left over after a day's work simply to recover.

Developing no goals or objectives for our leisure means only that nothing much will happen, and what does happen will be largely left to chance. Is this how we want to spend the equivalent of some twenty-five years of our lives?

Myth #4: The busiest and most active people achieve the most success.

If we have no plan or goals for our spare time, we will probably begin to feel uncomfortable after a while. Humans are goal-oriented creatures who quickly become upset or even physically ill without a sense of purpose. What happens, then, if we have no sense of purpose or direction for our leisure? We start to do things—anything—to keep busy and maintain our sanity. We join organizations. We take a second job or work longer hours on our first job. We continually seek out something to occupy our time. In short, we do anything we can to keep busy and escape from the discomfort of free time.

But merely keeping busy by burying ourselves in our work or a purposeless string of activities will do little to promote success or happiness in our lives.

Myth #5: Everything should be fun.

With so much emphasis in our society today on having a good time, we are always checking out our own moods. If we're not constantly smiling or laughing, we begin to suspect something is wrong with us. On the elevator, in the supermarket, and at the office, friends and strangers chide us to "smile" and "have fun." We worry and feel guilty even in our leisure time that we may not be having enough fun.

But genuine satisfaction and joy in living is not just going around with a happy smile plastered across your face or hopping from one so-called fun event to another to make sure we don't miss anything. Nor is it participating in every new fad that comes along or going to all the "in" places because everyone else is. True happiness grows from having thought through what we really want and care about and becoming involved in activities and with people because of a real interest. It is knowing what we want and patterning our lives accordingly, regardless of what the rest of the world is doing.

Myths about time and change

Myth #6: If only I had more will power, I could do whatever I wanted to do.

Many people believe that with enough will power, anything is possible. With more will power, I could get up earlier. I could organize my time better. I could stick to a diet. I could control my temper. I could stop procrastinating and finish all the projects I start. Over and over, the self-improvement books tell us to develop our ego strength, to be disciplined, and to muster up more will power. And we try. We make New Year's resolutions and have high hopes.

Myth #4: The busiest and most active people
achieve the most success

Does it work? Occasionally, sporadically, and inconsistently, depending on our mood, our habits, and a variety of other factors. In reality, the last thing you want to do is tell yourself that you *must* have more will power or that you *must* do something. When you tell yourself that you *must* do something, it sets up resistance. It backs you into a corner and makes what you are trying to do even *less* likely to occur. You do not have to have will power or be a superperson to achieve your goals and have more success. *There is an easier and much more effective route.*

Myth #7: We need to understand everything about ourselves before we can change significantly.

Many people believe that only when they know all about themselves will they be able to make substantial changes in themselves or improve their lot. They go all out to unravel the mysteries of their own minds and are constantly pondering why they think, feel, and act as they do. These are the "growth-group junkies," the "therapy-a-month" club members who spend the bulk of their leisure drifting from one workshop to another hoping to learn the "answers" about human nature.

But all the information about human behavior is not in, and it never will be. There are no final answers or set laws of behavior to discover. Fortunately, however, gaining insight into a few important principles of behavior *can* bring about significant and lasting changes in your life.

Myth #8: I have been this way so long it is virtually impossible to change.

Many of us reason that we have been the way we are for so many years that it is impossible for us to bring about any lasting changes in ourselves. The basis of this belief may be past failures that are then perpetuated by the thoughts you are feeding yourself. "I've *always* smoked too much," you tell yourself, "and even more so after that stop-smoking workshop I attended last spring." "I've *always* had a fear of flying; even thinking about a plane makes me nervous." "I've *always* been too passive with the opposite sex." "*Ever since I can remember* I've had a craving for sweets, in spite of my attempts to eat less." "I have been this way for so many years," you argue, "how could I possibly change?"

It takes a long time for any major changes to occur

But time, per se, has little to do with whether or not you can bring about changes for the better in yourself. It is the *procedures and knowledge* that you bring to your life *now* that make a difference.

Myth #9: It takes a long time for any major changes to occur.

Again, no. Given the right information and procedures, changes can come about very quickly. Furthermore, these need not be temporary, short-term superficial changes but can become a permanent part of your personality. This myth is related to the work-ethic notion which implies that for anything to be worthwhile it has to be a struggle. We think that in order to have the good things in life, be rewarded, and be the kind of person we want to be, we must go through some long, arduous, difficult process.

Nothing could be further from the truth. Important and lasting changes in your life can come about easily and surely without putting yourself through any long, painful, or complicated ordeal.

Myth #10: Personality is set by the age of five.

This is one of the most damaging of the neo-Freudian myths that many people believe. Often, it is a self-fulfilling prophecy: i.e., if you *believe* that something is predetermined according to your past experiences, most likely it will come about. However, this is because we *are* subject to the influence of our present thoughts and expectations, if not to those of our distant past.

Happily, this myth is false and can be discarded along with the others. People can change and grow in new directions throughout the life span, whether eighteen years old or eighty. It does not make any difference how rotten your life was during its first five years, in your teens, or even yesterday. What matters is what you do *today*.

Myth #11: Everything is fate.

This myth continues to hamper some of the most intelligent minds. "It all depends on circumstances," we hear over and over. "Most things that happen to us depend on events outside of our control." "Nothing I do seems to make any difference." "What I need is more luck in my life."

Myth #10: Personality is set by the age of five

In an era of social and economic troubles, a general pessimism and defeatism carries over into every aspect of our lives, whether within the political sphere, or the realm of our own personal lives. But every problem or crisis is an opportunity for positively changing the course of events. If we do not play an active role in bringing about change in our world, then we will no doubt be passive recipients of whatever life dishes out. But the choice is ours.

5.
Your Leisure Patterns

To be able to fill leisure intelligently is the last product of civilization.

—Bertrand Russell

The seven explorations in this chapter are designed to help you discover those leisure patterns best suited to your personality and become more aware of some specific ways in which your spare time may be slipping away from you. You will see how you fare in your personal relationships and whether too many of the wrong people are intruding on your time. Two of the exercises let you access your leisure dimensions and motivations so that you can more clearly see what changes you might want to make here. A self-exploration on the work/leisure dichotomy highlights whether your leisure is meeting important needs that are not being met on the job. Finally, suggestions are given on how to have more spare time by effectively resolving time-consuming conflicts and emotional downs. A sixteen-point "Up Your Energy" checklist provides guidelines for stamping out procrastination and inertia and realizing more zest.

Exploration #1: How do your leisure activities match up with your enjoyment?

Social scientists have found that there is often an inverse relationship between what we do in our spare time and what we actually enjoy doing. You may be participating in a number of activities that you do not especially enjoy, or, conversely, not doing many things that you would find satisfying. Clients typically tell me that they enjoy doing artwork, playing a musical instrument, or scuba diving more than anything else, only to realize that they haven't tried their hand at art in three years and haven't played a musical instrument or gone scuba-diving since they were children.

Similarly, clients will explain how they continue to play bridge, go bowling, watch television, or go out drinking week after week although they derive little enjoyment from these activities. Reasons will vary. Mostly their explanations point to a lackadaisical attitude toward the use of time and its value in their lives.

In taking stock of your use of spare time, ask yourself, "What activities and events in my life are rewarding, stimulating, or in some way satisfying?" Going to plays, reading, conversation with friends, biking, sports? The list is endless. Then take a look at the way you spend the bulk of your time. Is this what you want to do? What changes might you make?

Sometimes we do not know what we would like to do. If this is the case for you, think back over the activities in your life since you were a child. What have you done or thought about doing that really sparked your interest? Then make a commitment to yourself to explore those areas that *you* believe are important and re-creative—not those that others might think you should be doing.

Complete the Leisure-Time Activities Schedule, which begins on page 57 to discover how your participation in different activities aligns with your enjoyment. You may learn some surprising things about your use—or misuse—of leisure time!

We continue in activities that we no longer enjoy

LEISURE-TIME ACTIVITIES SCHEDULE

Instructions: Below is a list of activities. On the left side of the page, put a circle around the number that tells how often you participate in each activity, using the key at the top of the column. On the right side of the page, put a circle around the number that tells how much you enjoy doing each of these activities, using the key at the top of the column. If you never do the activity listed, circle 1 in the left-hand column and rate how much you think you would like it in the right-hand column.

Although this looks like a lengthy list, it should only take you a few minutes. Go through it quickly, then use the directions at the end to see how you fared.

Participation

1 Never
2 Rarely
3 Occasionally
4 Fairly often
5 Frequently

Enjoyment

1 Dislike very much
2 Dislike
3 Indifferent
4 Like
5 Like very much

Participation	Activity	Enjoyment
1 ②3 4 5	1. Bicycling	1 2 ③④ 5
①② 3 4 5	2. Cooking/Baking	1②③ 4 5
①2 3 4 5	3. Playing football	①2 ③ 4 5
①2 ③4 5	4. Hunting	①2③4 5
①2 ③4 5	5. Painting/Drawing	1 2③④ 5
①2 ③4 5	6. Scuba diving	1 2③4⑤
1 2 3④5	7. Partying	1 2 3④5
1②3 ④5	8. Watching TV programs	1 2③④5
①2 3 4 5	9. Playing basketball	①2 3 4 5
①②3 4 5	10. Chess	1②③4 5
①2 3 4 5	11. Flying/Gliding	1 2③4 5
①2 ③4 5	12. Horseback riding	①2 3④5
①2 3 4 5	13. Motorcycling	1②③④4 5
1 2 3④5	14. Window-shopping	1 2③④5
1 2③4⑤	15. Visiting friends	1 2 3④5
①②3 4 5	16. Writing poetry/stories	①2 3 4 5
①②3 4 5	17. Playing baseball/softball	1 2③4 5
1 2③④5	18. Backgammon	1 2③④5
①②3 4 5	19. Fishing: fresh water	1 2③4 5
①2③4 5	20. Fishing: salt water	1 2③4 5

1 2 3 4 5	21. Hiking	1 2 3 4 5
1 2 3 4 5	22. Walking	1 2 3 4 5
1 2 3 4 5	23. Model-building	1 2 3 4 5
1 2 3 4 5	24. Playing golf	1 2 3 4 5
1 2 3 4 5	25. Dancing: ballet, modern jazz, etc.	1 2 3 4 5
1 2 3 4 5	26. Social dancing	1 2 3 4 5
1 2 3 4 5	27. Tennis	1 2 3 4 5
1 2 3 4 5	28. Encounter groups	1 2 3 4 5
1 2 3 4 5	29. Singing	1 2 3 4 5
1 2 3 4 5	30. Badminton	1 2 3 4 5
1 2 3 4 5	31. Ceramics/Pottery	1 2 3 4 5
1 2 3 4 5	32. Exercising	1 2 3 4 5
1 2 3 4 5	33. Mechanics	1 2 3 4 5
1 2 3 4 5	34. Table tennis	1 2 3 4 5
1 2 3 4 5	35. Viewing wrestling/boxing	1 2 3 4 5
1 2 3 4 5	36. Attending large social functions (balls, benefit programs, etc.)	1 2 3 4 5
1 2 3 4 5	37. Attending small social gatherings (dinner parties, etc.)	1 2 3 4 5
1 2 3 4 5	38. Sailing	1 2 3 4 5
1 2 3 4 5	39. Canoeing	1 2 3 4 5
1 2 3 4 5	40. Motor boating	1 2 3 4 5
1 2 3 4 5	41. Gambling	1 2 3 4 5
1 2 3 4 5	42. Electronics	1 2 3 4 5
1 2 3 4 5	43. Gymnastics	1 2 3 4 5
1 2 3 4 5	44. Listening to records	1 2 3 4 5
1 2 3 4 5	45. Sewing	1 2 3 4 5
1 2 3 4 5	46. Swimming	1 2 3 4 5
1 2 3 4 5	47. Sunbathing/Going to the beach	1 2 3 4 5
1 2 3 4 5	48. Auto repairing	1 2 3 4 5
1 2 3 4 5	49. Carpentry/Handicrafts	1 2 3 4 5
1 2 3 4 5	50. Driving (other than for work)	1 2 3 4 5
1 2 3 4 5	51. Leather working	1 2 3 4 5
1 2 3 4 5	52. Surfing (body or board)	1 2 3 4 5
1 2 3 4 5	53. Weight lifting	1 2 3 4 5
1 2 3 4 5	54. Auto racing	1 2 3 4 5
1 2 3 4 5	55. Listening to radio: music	1 2 3 4 5
1 2 3 4 5	56. Listening to radio: news	1 2 3 4 5
1 2 3 4 5	57. Listening to radio: sports	1 2 3 4 5
1 2 3 4 5	58. Camping	1 2 3 4 5

1 2 3 4 5	59. Dining out	1 2 3 4 5
1 2 3 4 5	60. Going to plays	1 2 3 4 5
1 2 3 4 5	61. Knitting/Crocheting	1 2 3 4 5
1 2 3 4 5	62. Reading: plays, poetry	1 2 3 4 5
1 2 3 4 5	63. Water-skiing	1 2 3 4 5
1 2 3 4 5	64. Travel	1 2 3 4 5
1 2 3 4 5	65. Attending lectures (not college)	1 2 3 4 5
1 2 3 4 5	66. Social clubs	1 2 3 4 5
1 2 3 4 5	67. Taking college courses	1 2 3 4 5
1 2 3 4 5	68. Playing poker	1 2 3 4 5
1 2 3 4 5	69. Playing a musical instrument	1 2 3 4 5
1 2 3 4 5	70. Going to nightclubs	1 2 3 4 5
1 2 3 4 5	71. Wrestling/Boxing	1 2 3 4 5
1 2 3 4 5	72. Reading magazines	1 2 3 4 5
1 2 3 4 5	73. Playing bridge	1 2 3 4 5
1 2 3 4 5	74. Gardening	1 2 3 4 5
1 2 3 4 5	75. Jogging	1 2 3 4 5
1 2 3 4 5	76. Sightseeing	1 2 3 4 5
1 2 3 4 5	77. Games of chance	1 2 3 4 5
1 2 3 4 5	78. Going to movies	1 2 3 4 5
1 2 3 4 5	79. Reading newspaper: editorial section	1 2 3 4 5
1 2 3 4 5	80. Reading newspaper: book review section	1 2 3 4 5
1 2 3 4 5	81. Reading newspaper: sports section	1 2 3 4 5
1 2 3 4 5	82. Reading newspaper: financial section	1 2 3 4 5
1 2 3 4 5	83. Reading newspaper: theater/movie critiques	1 2 3 4 5
1 2 3 4 5	84. Reading newspaper: front page	1 2 3 4 5
1 2 3 4 5	85. Flower arranging	1 2 3 4 5
1 2 3 4 5	86. Weaving/Needlework	1 2 3 4 5
1 2 3 4 5	87. Judo/Karate	1 2 3 4 5
1 2 3 4 5	88. Human growth groups	1 2 3 4 5
1 2 3 4 5	89. Political activities	1 2 3 4 5
1 2 3 4 5	90. Viewing documentary films	1 2 3 4 5
1 2 3 4 5	91. Jewelry making	1 2 3 4 5
1 2 3 4 5	92. Bowling	1 2 3 4 5
1 2 3 4 5	93. Acting/Dramatics	1 2 3 4 5
1 2 3 4 5	94. Business/Professional Organizations	1 2 3 4 5
1 2 3 4 5	95. Attending conferences/conventions	1 2 3 4 5
1 2 3 4 5	96. Reading books: fiction	1 2 3 4 5

1 2 3 4 5	97. Reading books: nonfiction	1 2 3 4 5
1 2 3 4 5	98. Meditation	1 2 3 4 5
1 2 3 4 5	99. Going to basketball games	1 2 3 4 5
1 2 3 4 5	100. Going to football games	1 2 3 4 5
1 2 3 4 5	101. Going to baseball/softball games	1 2 3 4 5
1 2 3 4 5	102. Watching TV: team sports	1 2 3 4 5
1 2 3 4 5	103. Watching TV: news	1 2 3 4 5
1 2 3 4 5	104. Watching TV: programs on foreign affairs	1 2 3 4 5
1 2 3 4 5	105. Watching TV: panel discussions on current issues	1 2 3 4 5
1 2 3 4 5	106. Browsing in the library	1 2 3 4 5
1 2 3 4 5	107. Conservation/Ecology organizations	1 2 3 4 5
1 2 3 4 5	108. Religious organizations	1 2 3 4 5
1 2 3 4 5	109. Playing the stock market	1 2 3 4 5
1 2 3 4 5	110. Visiting museums	1 2 3 4 5
1 2 3 4 5	111. Playing volleyball	1 2 3 4 5
1 2 3 4 5	112. Snorkeling	1 2 3 4 5
1 2 3 4 5	113. Social drinking	1 2 3 4 5
1 2 3 4 5	114. Gossiping	1 2 3 4 5
1 2 3 4 5	115. Computer games	1 2 3 4 5
1 2 3 4 5	116. Writing: letters	1 2 3 4 5
1 2 3 4 5	117. Bird watching	1 2 3 4 5
1 2 3 4 5	118. Getting stoned	1 2 3 4 5
1 2 3 4 5	119. Squash/Handball	1 2 3 4 5
1 2 3 4 5	120. Metalwork	1 2 3 4 5
1 2 3 4 5	121. Arguing	1 2 3 4 5
1 2 3 4 5	122. Sexual activity	1 2 3 4 5
1 2 3 4 5	123. Billiards/Pool	1 2 3 4 5
1 2 3 4 5	124. Exchanging ideas with others	1 2 3 4 5
1 2 3 4 5	125. Solving puzzles	1 2 3 4 5
1 2 3 4 5	126. Family visiting	1 2 3 4 5
1 2 3 4 5	127. Attending concerts (not rock)	1 2 3 4 5
1 2 3 4 5	128. Attending concerts (rock)	1 2 3 4 5
1 2 3 4 5	129. Sitting and thinking	1 2 3 4 5
1 2 3 4 5	130. Special hobbies: stamps, photography, amateur radio, etc.	1 2 3 4 5
1 2 3 4 5	131. Telephone visiting	1 2 3 4 5
1 2 3 4 5	132. Racquetball	1 2 3 4 5

How to score your Leisure-Time Activities Schedule

1. Pinpoint any discrepancies between what you enjoy doing but are not by circling those activities for which your Enjoyment score is 4 or 5 (*Like* or *Like very much*), but your Participation score is only 1 or 2 (*Never* or *Rarely*). *How many activities are you neglecting that could be a potential source of pleasure and satisfaction?*
2. Next, identify those activities that you are involved in but dislike by placing a check mark beside activities for which your Participation score is 4 or 5 (*Fairly often* or *Frequently*) but your Enjoyment score is only 1 or 2 (*Dislike very much* or *Dislike*). *How many activities are you caught up in that you do not really enjoy?*

If by chance you found few pastimes that you were interested in, take a look at the Activity List below for some more intriguing kinds of activities. Use it to whet your appetite to the many possibilities.

MORE ACTIVITIES

The extent of leisure activities is limited only by our imaginations. Let the list below act as a stimulus to the many possibilities. Check off any that you would be interested in pursuing.

1. Whale watching
2. Ice fishing
3. Spearfishing
4. Windsurfing
5. Waterfall walking
6. Drag-boat racing
7. Exploring sea caves
8. Inner-tube floating
9. Raft trips
10. Wallowing in hot mineral springs
11. Immersions: mud, wine, oatmeal
12. Belly dancing
13. Animal mimicry
14. Fox hunting
15. Bobsledding
16. Sky-diving
17. Playing polo
18. Intellectual jogging
19. Storytelling
20. Doing diary fantasies
21. Worm grunting
22. Freighter trips
23. Kite racing
24. Hang-gliding
25. Jumping rope
26. Steamboat cruises
27. Sport parachuting
28. Parasailing
29. Roller coasting
30. Chasing eclipses

31. Tree climbing
32. Orienteering
33. Panning
34. Cross-country skiing
35. Hot-dog skiing
36. Skibobbing
37. Surfing
38. Sand sailing
39. Downhill biking
40. Desert racing
41. Hot-air ballooning
42. Watching meteor showers
43. Joining a birding team

44. Horseback riding through a volcano
45. Curling (shuffleboard on ice)
46. Blackpowder shooting
47. A sewer tour
48. Downhill rolling
49. Overhead people-passing
50. Group juggling
51. Frisbee golf
52. City walks
53. River walks
54. Watching a sunrise

Exploration #2: What is your Time-and-People Picture?

If you were to list the most important people in your life, who would they be and how much time are you spending with them? It is easy to get ourselves into situations where the wrong people are taking up too much of our time.

A neighbor may telephone "just to chat" when you are right in the middle of a project. A casual acquaintance may drop in and disrupt your day because she or he has nothing better to do. And the minutes and hours lost in this way can add up. Why do we let it happen? It can be for any number of reasons. Perhaps we worry about hurting the intruder's feelings. We may rationalize that what we are doing at the time we're interrupted is not all that important anyway. The main reason, however, is that most of us have no definite plans or schedules for much of our spare time, and so we easily fall into doing what others want us to do.

At work, most of us carefully plan our day and set schedules and deadlines for ourselves. Yet in our personal relationships our time is frequently up for grabs. We meet people and spend time with others largely by chance. And we usually date and marry the people we just happen to come in contact with. We rarely explore all the social options open to us or make a systematic attempt to consider what might be more in keeping with our values, interests, and needs. Sometimes our haphazard approach works out well, but sometimes it doesn't.

However, it is not just the time that we spend with others that matters but the quality of that time. Is it stimulating, exciting, enjoyable? Is it a growth experience wherein we learn through open communication and sharing? Is it based on mutual respect, love, and understanding? Or is it frequently filled with bitterness, hostility, misunderstanding, competition, jealousy, and frustration?

Take a moment to consider the people in your life. Is the quality of the time you spend with them what you would like it to be? Are you spending too much time with people out of obligation or habit, or with people you have outgrown and whose company you no longer enjoy?

If you do not place a premium on your time, no one else is likely to.

Complete the Time-and-People-Picture exercise on page 64 to raise your awareness of who you are spending your time with, how often, and their relative importance to your life.

Exploration #3: Are your present dimensions of leisure right for you?

What we do in our leisure time—that time when we are freest to be ourselves—is an expression of our values and our priorities.

Are the leisure dimensions of your life consistent with the way you see yourself and want to be? If not, what changes might you make? Here are some of the questions to consider in addressing this fundamental issue.

Do you find that you are more of a *spectator* or a *participant?*

Are most of your activities *competitive* or *cooperative?*

Do you prefer *individual* sports or *team* sports? (Among women, personality differences have been found between athletes engaged in individual sports and team sports. Women in individual sports tend to be more dominant, self-sufficient, and impulsive. They tend to be self-assured and have stronger emotional, artistic, and creative interests. They are also more radical in their thinking and less inhibited. Team-sports athletes, on the other hand, are more steady, practical, dependable, and emotionally disciplined. Women from both groups are intellectually brighter, more conscientious, aggressive, and persevering than nonathletic groups. Socially, they are somewhat cool and aloof.)[1]

---

1. *S. L. Peterson, J. C. Weber, and W. W. Trousdale, "Personality Traits of Women in Team Sports vs. Women in Individual Sports,"* Research Quarterly of the American Association for Health and Physical Education, *Vol. 38 (1967), pp. 686-690.*

YOUR TIME-AND-PEOPLE PICTURE

Instructions: List below the people (friends, family, acquaintances, and strangers) whom you are spending most of your spare time with. Estimate the number of hours per week you spend with each and their degree of importance to your life. A is high, F is low. Include telephone time as well as time spent in communication by letter or computer chatting.

Names	Contact time (Hrs. per week)	Importance
1. STEVE	4	C
2. DEIRDRE	28	B
3. JEFFER	10	A
4. LIBBY	10	B
5. ALLISON	12	B
6. THERESA	5	F
7. LOU	7	C
8. MOM/DAD	2	A
9. MARTA	4	B
TIM	6	B

Analysis of Your Time-and-People Picture: Make a note of those people whom you are spending the bulk of your time with. Ask yourself if you are spending too much time with some people at the expense of others who hold a more important place in your life.

What sports in particular do you enjoy? Personality differences have been found among those who participate in various sports. Fencers are more dominating than basketball players, volleyball players, or boxers. Badminton players have been judged to be the most extroverted group, while volleyball players are more emotionally unstable. Male sky-divers, snow skiers, and scuba divers, however, describe themselves as socially abrasive and calm.[2]

Do you find that most of your free time is spent *indoors* or *outdoors?* Do you like mental games such as chess, backgammon, and cards, or are physical sports more to your liking? (A number of differences have been found between sport-loving and nonsport-loving groups.) Male skiers tend to be less tense and less irritable and to have calmer, more confident personalities than nonathletic males. Varsity athletes have been found to be lower in anxiety than nonathletes. Major-league baseball players appear to have more self-discipline, initiative, and ability to get along with others than minor-league players.[3]

Is most of your spare time spent *alone* or with *others?* How is your time divided between your family and friends?

Do you plan many of your leisure hours, or are most of the things you do in your spare time left to chance? (A recent study has suggested that leisure activities are more likely to be planned by people with more integrated, abstract personalities.[4])

Do you find that most of your spare time is spent in *modern* or in *traditional* kinds of events? Do you prefer conventional or unconventional pastimes? Do you get caught up in leisure fads?

What role does risk play in your leisure life style? Risk includes physical, emotional, and intellectual risk. Some people find hand-gliding, mountain climbing, and sky-diving to their liking, but approach close emotional relationships with fear and anxiety. Some cannot resist the challenge of a puzzle or a mental problem but avoid any physical adventure such as river rafting or hot-air ballooning.

---

2. **L. A. Flanagan, "A Study of Some Personality Traits of Different Physical Activity Groups," Research Quarterly, Vol. 22 (1951), pp. 312-323. W. S. Martin and F. L. Myrick, "Personality and Leisure Time Activities," Research Quarterly, Vol. 47 (2), pp. 246-253.
3. E. G. Booth, Jr., "Personality Traits of Athletes as Measured by the MMPI," Research Quarterly, Vol. 29 (1958), pp. 127-138; J. P. LaPlace, "Personality and Its Relationship to Success in Professional Baseball, Research Quarterly, Vol. 22 (1951), pp. 312-323.
4. J. L. Gault, "Leisure Behavior as a Function of Cognitive Personality Variables," Ph.D. Dissertation, 1978, p. 114.

Related to this is the choice between *structured* and *nonstructured* activities. Many people prefer a structured situation where they know the rules and exactly what is expected of them, rather than coping with the uncertainty of an unstructured situation. An example would be taking a guided tour where hotel accommodations, meals, and sightseeing are set up in advance as compared with traveling alone and making the arrangements on the spot. Another example would be participating in a game with definite rules as compared with being in an encounter group where the rules are not clearly defined.

As you can see, your personality is closely bound up with the varieties of leisure activity you prefer. Complete the Dimensions of Leisure chart on page 67. It will help you more fully understand the kinds of activities best suited to your personality.

Exploration #4: What motivates you in your leisure?

It is helpful to look at not only *what* we do in our free time but *why*. What are the motivations behind our pastimes? We may participate in different activities for any number of reasons, and gain various benefits from them. One person may jog for physical fitness—to increase blood circulation, lose weight, or ward off a heart attack. Another person may jog because "everyone's doing it," even though she does not especially enjoy it. Still another may take up jogging because of pressure to exercise from his or her mate.

We join civic organizations out of social concern and because we want to help bring about changes in society. We join clubs to meet people socially, to make friends, and to establish business contacts. We may travel to a foreign country out of curiosity, to broaden our experiences, or as an escape from boredom. We may go to the movies to be entertained or because someone we like to be with has invited us. We attend classes and lectures to advance our career, for mental stimulation, for personal growth, or for the rewards that might come from receiving a degree. We may watch television as a means of escape or because we find it relaxing. Playing tennis or racketball might be for exercise or for the self-esteem that comes from winning. We may spend all of our spare time charting commodity trends on our home computer because we want to achieve financial independence, for the fun of it, or for both reasons.

Think about the pastimes you are involved in. What percentage of your time do you spend on activities for physical fitness? For personal

DIMENSIONS OF LEISURE

Instructions: What percentage of your leisure activities fall along the dimensions below? Indicate your estimate on the scales by drawing a line between 0 and 100%.

1. **Indoors**_____|_____**Outdoors**
   0%   100%

2. **Alone**_____|_____**With others**
   0%   100%

3. **Planned**_____|_____**Spontaneous**
   0%   100%

4. **Family**_____|_____**Friends**
   0%   100%

5. **Competitive**___|_____**Cooperative**
   0%   100%

6. **Mental**_____|_____**Physical**
   0%   100%

7. **Observer**_____|_____**Participant**
   0%   100%

8. **Stimulating**_____|_____**Relaxing**
   0%   100%

9. **Simple**_____|_____**Difficult**
   0%   100%

10. **Modern**_____|_____**Traditional**
    0%   100%

11. **Conventional**_____|_____**Nonconventional**
    0%   100%

12. **Structured**_____|_____**Nonstructured**
    0%   100%

growth? As a creative outlet? For relaxation? And how much time is spent out of boredom, or because of demands and pressures from others? Chart your answers on the Leisure Motivations Profile on page 69.

A typical motivational profile (although no one pattern is truly "typical") might show 5 percent of one's time spent for physical fitness, 10 percent for mental stimulation, 30 percent to relax, 45 percent due to pressure from others, and 15 percent for personal growth. Each person is unique, however; there are no right or wrong patterns. The only criterion is, "What is right for you?" Ask yourself what makes the most sense from where you stand. How does your profile align with your values and objectives? What changes would you like to make? Are you spending enough time for relaxation? Would you like to have more time for personal growth and creativity? It is not so much *what* you are doing that makes a difference in your life, but the benefits you are receiving—or failing to enjoy.

Exploration #5: How do your leisure and work correspond?

One way to look at leisure is in relation to work, since how you spend your working hours will determine to some extent how your leisure time is used.

The linkages between leisure and work are many, and can be both positive and negative. On the positive side, whatever your work fails to provide, leisure can compensate for. Some questions to ask yourself are these: What needs are being met or not met by your occupation? Does your work offer opportunities for creativity? Are you under a lot of pressure during working hours? Is a large portion of your work tedious or routine? Is your work primarily physically demanding or mentally demanding?

In other words, it is important to recognise how your work is or is not contributing to your overall well-being. If your occupation is tedious and monotonous, you may seek stimulation in leisure. On the other hand, if you are under a lot of pressure during working hours, quieter, relaxing forms of leisure might be sought.

To help you assess those needs that your work is meeting or not meeting, and that leisure might compensate for, complete the Work/Leisure Grid on page 70.

LEISURE MOTIVATIONS PROFILE

Instructions: Below is a list of possible reasons why you might participate in different leisure activities. Estimate what percentage of your leisure time is spent according to each of these functions. Your total percentage of time will likely add up to over 100 percent, since many activities serve several functions (e.g., you may run for fitness as well as for fun and relaxation). Then consider how you would prefer to be spending your time.

	Estimated Percentage of Time	Percentage of Time I'd Prefer
Physical fitness	2	10
Mental stimulation	2	20
Fun	5	20
Relaxation	10	50
Being creative	~~5 10~~	30
Out of social concern	10	30
Affiliation	5	10
Pressure from others	10	15
Just something to do	10	20
Entertainment	5	30
Escape from boredom	5	10
Social/Business contacts	5	30
Personal growth	5	30
Variety	10	30
Self-esteem	5	20
Recognition	5	40
Curiosity	10	40

YOUR WORK/LEISURE GRID

Instructions: First, rate your job on how well it is meeting the personal needs listed below. Use this key:

1 Almost never
2 Rarely
③ Occasionally
4 Fairly often
5 Almost always

Now go through the needs again and rate your leisure on each. Also rate how important each need is to you. A is high, F is low.

Personal Needs	My work provides	My leisure provides	Degree of importance to me
Mental challenge	B/A	D	B
Self-expression	B/A	D	B
Recognition	B	D	B
Personal development	C	D	B
Relaxation	D	B	B
Creativity	B	D	B
Good communication	B	D	B
Prestige	B	D	B
Self-esteem	B	D	B
Physical well-being	D	B	B
Enjoyment	C	B	B

Analysis of Your Work/Leisure Grid: How many important needs not met in the work setting are being met during your leisure hours? Is your leisure compensating for your work's shortcomings?

Sometimes our leisure does not compensate for the shortcomings of our occupations. Instead, work conditions are simply replicated in our leisure habits. Bored and discontented with our work, we carry our frustrations home with us, taking them out on our spouse, our children, or whoever happens to be handy. After spending eight hours sitting at a desk doing tedious, routine tasks, instead of seeking out stimulating or active leisure pastimes we come home, plop into a chair, and belt down two martinis or escape into home-video movies.

As you take stock of your use of time, ask yourself whether you have become too dependent upon unsatisfying, work-extending hobbies. How much of your leisure is spent in mere recuperation from work and in escape activities? Instead of providing new meaning for your life, does your leisure only reflect the loss of meaning in your work? What changes might you make to establish a more satisfactory balance between work and leisure?

In Western society, we use much of our spare time to advance our work interests. What proportion of your leisure time is spent in establishing or wooing business contacts? Do you feel anxious or guilty if you are not constantly busy doing something even in your leisure? Are you able to relax and clear your head of work projects after you leave the office? Do you believe that your free time is best used to serve your work interests?

There are no right or wrong answers to these questions. They are to be considered only to clarify what is best for you. If spending all your spare time making business contacts is consistent with your values and goals at this time, then that is exactly what you need to be doing.

Leisure and work have a dynamic two-way relationship. Changes in your work can result in changes in your leisure pastimes, and vice versa, according to your own personality.

Exploration #6: Is your handling of your emotions getting you down?

Much of our misuse of time is due to obsolete thought modes and faulty emotional patterns. We are often dominated by thought patterns that have long been antiquated. In spite of our desire to conduct our affairs rationally and keep our emotional equilibrium, a swirl of emotions often takes over our lives. We lash out in anger. We feel despair, frustration, and anguish. This drains us of energy and stifles

Is your emotional time space keeping you upset?

our enthusiasm and zest for living. Isn't there an easier way to deal with problems? Yes, there is.

Our emotions are to a large extent a by-product of our systems of thought and beliefs. Changing our thinking can change our feelings and moods. The goal is not to eliminate emotion from our lives but to recognize how cues act to elicit our feelings and how their expression affects us. Then we have a choice: to be angry, hostile, anxious, guilty, resentful, hurt—or not. The question is: Is it worth it? Is expressing our anger (or bitterness, resentment, and so on) interfering with our objectives or advancing them? Is it draining our energy and wasting time? Is it costing us more than its payoff value?

These issues are so important that we will consider them at some length.

The myth of catharsis

Whenever I talk to clients or students about *choosing* our emotional responses according to the outcome we want, someone usually raises this objection: "But we can't keep our feelings all inside us. If we feel angry or upset, we need to express it, to get it out of our system; otherwise it may fester and churn inside and perhaps even cause an ulcer. *Better to get it out and get it over with."* And this would make sense if in fact that is what happened. But, unfortunately, acting out your anger, screaming, ranting, raving, charging up your blood pressure, and coming in for the kill like a wild boar *does not get rid of the anger.* The anger may subside for a time, possibly due to fatigue, but it is ready to erupt again unexpectedly, given the right cue.

What you are actually doing when you let your emotions get out of hand is *reinforcing* your anger, refueling it for an even greater effect the next time around.

The idea of catharsis—the purging of emotion to release tension— is, therefore, merely a myth. This has been confirmed by hundreds of empirical studies and personal experiences. However, we still see popular therapy groups encouraging their members to act out aggressive and hostile feelings through screaming at the top of their lungs, beating inanimate objects with all their might, and engaging in violent person-to-person encounters. Think about it. Have angry quarrels with your mate or others *lessened* the likelihood of future angry encounters? Probably not. The best you can hope for is a temporary feeling of relief, with future fights usually growing even more intense and out of control. Only when we come to terms with the *thinking processes* that prompted the emotional outburst can we bring about changes to produce the consequences we desire.

Faulty emotional patterns

Frequently, faulty emotional patterns are established in early childhood. Perhaps you discovered as a young child that getting angry got you what you wanted. Whenever you threw a temper tantrum, if you laid it on long and hard enough, you got your way. Today that same mode of response lingers on, even though it is rarely effective in bringing about the outcome you would like.

One of my former clients, Martin, a young insurance executive, provides a typical example. He and his family had been planning a vacation for months. Work had been hectic, and they were looking forward to having some fun and relaxation for a couple of weeks. They decided to fly to Oahu, Hawaii, and stay at a hotel in Kahala.

Upon arriving at the airport, they located a taxi and were taken to their destination, only to find that the driver had apparently overcharged them. What did Martin do? He lashed out and put the driver on the defensive. The inevitable nasty scene occurred. Martin's behavior was reflexive, automatically following from his thoughts that ran something like, "Damn taxi drivers, always trying to rip off the tourists—I'm not going to let him get away with this!" The consequences were quite predictable. He provoked the driver's wrath, a big argument resulted, his wife became irritable, the baby started crying, and a minor incident was blown up way out of proportion. Was it worth it?

It is not unusual for many tourists to go through their vacations frustrated and upset because of things that go wrong. Vacation time with its lack of routine and unsettling surprises, coupled with our often unrealistically high expectations of fun, can make us especially prone to irritability. Sometimes this happens simply because we have selected a vacation spot and activities unsuited to our personality and interests.

No matter how much planning we do, things will often go wrong, whether we are on vacation, at home, or at work. Things never turn out quite as we would like them. People are not always fair, and sometimes they are outright scoundrels. But why let this disrupt our lives and our peace of mind any more than necessary?

This is not to say that there will not be times when you will get upset or blow up. But you can control how often this happens and what consequences it has. In taking stock of your emotional time, estimate what percentage of your time you feel angry, enervated, bored, or apathetic. How often do you feel worried, anxious, and insecure? How much of your time is filled with jealousy, suspicion, and frustration?

Compare this "downtime" with the amount of "uptime" when you are feeling energized, enthusiastic, and confident. What percentage of time do you feel elated, joyful, and inspired? What portion of your life is filled with love and trust?

Do the Emotional-Time-Space exercises below to crystalize and assess your emotional patterns. Then look at the Up Your Energy checklist beginning on page 76 for sixteen suggestions on how to enhance your emotional well-being.

YOUR EMOTIONAL-TIME-SPACE

Instructions: Our emotions are to a large extent a function of our beliefs and thought resources. On the scales below, estimate where you are in your emotional time-space.

Scale 1: Assessment of Downtime

Rate yourself from 0% to 100%. What percentage
of your time do you feel:

1. Enervated	_____%
2. Worried	_____%
3. Depressed	_____%
4. Anxious	_____%
5. Bored	_____%
6. Hostile	_____%
7. Angry	_____%
8. Jealous	_____%
9. Apathetic	_____%
10. Suspicious	_____%
11. Frustrated	_____%
12. Insecure	_____%

Overall average downtime rating

_____%

Scale 2: Assessment of Uptime

Rate yourself from 0% to 100%. What percentage
of your time do you feel:

1.	Energized	_____%
2.	Hopeful	_____%
3.	Enthusiastic	_____%
4.	Confident	_____%
5.	Elated	_____%
6.	Trustful	_____%
7.	Relaxed	_____%
8.	Amiable	_____%
9.	Inspired	_____%
10.	Loving	_____%
11.	Secure	_____%
12.	Concerned	_____%

Overall average uptime rating

_____%

Analysis of Your Emotional-Time-Space: How does your amount of
uptime compare with your amount of downtime? What changes
would you like to make?

UP YOUR ENERGY

Checklist for Reduction of Worry, Inertia, and Procrastination

- *Be task-oriented.* When something is bothering you, try to identify
  specifically what it is, face it squarely, and make a *start* toward its
  resolution.
- *Stop brooding.* Recognize that continually feeding yourself negative
  thoughts will keep you down and out. Stop telling yourself the car
  needs repairs, the costs of groceries are outrageous, your job is
  lousy, your mate no longer loves you, ad infinitum.
- *Make a list of all the good things in your life.* Keep it where you'll see it
  often: on the wall by your bed, in your purse or wallet, on your desk.
  Be reminded that things aren't *all* bad.

- *Fill your mind with happy thoughts.* Repeat positive affirmations while you're jogging, waiting for a bus, or commuting. Dream some happy plans.
- *Laugh.* Try not to take life so seriously. Go out and be around some happy people, listen to a funny TV show or lecture. Play a comedy record, write a hilarious letter or poem.
- *Move about.* Worry clings to the sedentary soul. Walk around the block. Jump rope. Ride a bike. Skip. Stand on your head. Dance. Take a swim. Bend over and touch your toes a few times.
- *Do something new just for fun.* Try a new hobby, go to a different part of town, meet someone new, learn a dance step.
- *Straighten up.* How's your posture? When you slouch while sitting or standing, you put a strain on your body that can burn up energy and contribute to stress.
- *Check the air you're breathing.* Is it filled with smoke, smog, pollution, or air conditioning? Change the ion flow by adding plants, running water or a negative-ion generator to your home or office. This will help to keep you from feeling sluggish and burned out.
- *Pamper yourself.* Treat yourself to a lobster luncheon, buy yourself something special, take a bubble bath, try a new hair style, go to a fun seminar.
- *Get involved.* Joy in living comes from having a purpose and moving toward those goals consistent with your values. Work toward something you believe in.
- *Take a look at your diet.* Eating junk foods, sugar, white flour, preservatives, and chemical additives can upset your body chemistry and make you tense.
- *Do a few deep-breathing exercises.* Begin by forcefully exhaling all the air in your lungs. Next, inhale slowly and deeply through your nose, filling first your stomach, then your chest. Hold it to the count of three, then exhale slowly through your mouth. Do this several times and feel the tension leave your body.
- *Listen to some soothing meditation music.* Keep a cassette recorder handy and when you begin feeling rushed and out of sorts, lie back for a few minutes and let your head clear of all the tacky, busy thoughts invading your consciousness.
- *Rid your mind of nagging "should-do's".* Stop being dominated by all the things you should have done and didn't do (past) or should be doing and aren't (present). Realize that life is always half undone, and there will always be things left over. Make up a small, manageable "to do" list, take one item, and *do it now.*
- *Wake up to something pleasant.* Throw away the alarm clock. Wake

A "yes-yes" conflict

up to a cassette of happy affirmations or a favorite song. Try a nature recording with rippling water falls, birds singing, and wind rustling through the trees. Take charge of your mind in those early morning hours and your whole day will go a little better.

In the later chapters of this book, specific strategies will be given to help you minimize the self-defeating, debilitating emotions that may be resulting in procrastination and lack of energy and so crippling your leisure life style.

Exploration #7: Are you handling conflicts and making decisions effectively?

Indecision and vacillation sap our strength and are a number-one time waster. We are constantly confronted with choices, some minor, some major, and a few with great impact on our lives. These choices can lead to two kinds of internal conflicts: the "yes-yes" conflict (also called the "approach-approach" conflict) and the "no-no" conflict (also called the "avoidance-avoidance" conflict). The former involves making a choice between two or more things that we want when we can have only one. For example, we can go to the movies on Saturday night or attend a play, but not both. We want to have a child, but we also want freedom to travel and not be tied down. We would like to have two mates, Marlene and Nancy, but legally can have only one.

The second kind of conflict, the "no-no" conflict, requires making a choice between two things that we do *not* want to happen when we feel forced to settle on one of them. We can either drive to work in a traffic jam or take the commuter train, with its frequent breakdowns. We can either stay in a job we detest or go through the hassle of finding another one. We can continue to sleep on a lumpy mattress or go into debt to buy a new one. We can keep sharing our luxurious apartment with a noisy, obtrusive roommate, or live alone in a smaller, drab, inexpensive place.

"No-no" conflicts are the most difficult to handle and, until resolved, can keep us feeling anxious and despondent. In order to arrive at a solution, we may need to redefine the conflict and avoid the either-or trap we have set up for ourselves. Instead of either driving to work or taking the train, maybe we can live closer to work and walk or ride a bike. Perhaps we can work out of our home part of the week, as a growing number of people are doing. Or perhaps we can simply lessen the frustration of driving to work in traffic by listening to a

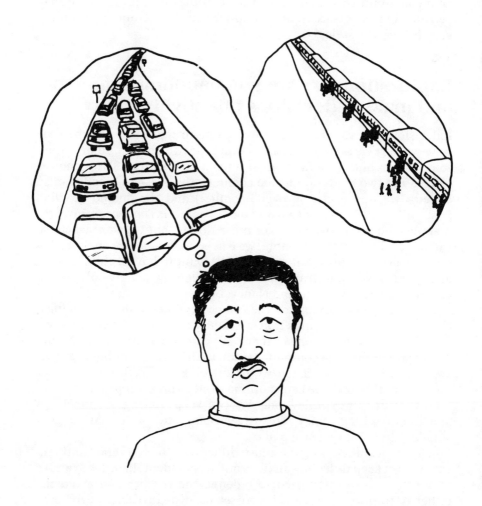

A 'no-no' conflict

lecture or book on cassette tape in our car. Rather than staying in a job we intensely dislike, we can seek out other positions and make our job search more an adventure than a chore. Instead of sleeping on a lumpy mattress, we might try putting boards under it or buying an inexpensive reupholstered one. When faced with a "no-no" conflict, by opening our minds to creative alternatives we can, to some extent, avoid locking ourselves into an unwanted outcome.

Most people have difficulty in making a decision. Training yourself to become a better decision-maker is one key to success. Here are a few typical reasons for indecisiveness and vacillation and what you can do about them.

Fear of the unpleasant consequences of making the wrong decision

Recognize that everyone makes mistakes. It has been said that "genius makes the most mistakes." A complete avoidance of mistakes generally means few decisions and an overly cautious, nonaction-oriented life style. Generally speaking, any decision is better than none at all. Even if you are right only 51 percent of the time, you can come out ahead.

Lack of a sound or systematic procedure for arriving at a decision.

Many of us delay making a decision in the hope that, by some miracle, inspiration will "hit" us and we'll know for certain that we have made the right choice. Recognize that this is black-white thinking. In most situations, any number of alternatives are usually workable; no one answer is necessarily best.

Attempting to gather too much information

Sometimes we try to gather too much information in relation to the importance of the decision. We arm ourselves with volumes of charts, facts, and data trying to make sure that we do not overlook anything. As important as good research is, it can be carried to an extreme. Try to balance the importance of the decision for your goals with the amount of time and effort expended on reaching the decision. There will always be additional information that could be gathered; there will always remain some degree of uncertainty. Obtain all the known and relevant information available within a specific time, and *then* *decide.*

Making a decision while under stress

Make the important decisions in your life from a clear and calm perspective. Never make crucial decisions when you are overly tired, drinking, on drugs, or in a highly charged emotional state, whether euphoric or upset. When you find yourself in a hyper-emotional state, postpone any major decisions until your head is clear and you are more composed. We do unbelievable damage to ourselves by some of the decisions we make when we are angry, upset, or despondent.

Times of decision are crucial in your life. Successful people are generally decisive people. Let everything you do be a result of *your* *decision* rather than of aimless drifting.

III
TAKING THE LEAP: CREATING THE LEISURE PATTERNS OF YOUR CHOICE

6.
The Power of Leisure Commitment

Leisure offers a marvelous opportunity for freedom to be exercised, but where there is no commitment that freedom becomes aimlessness or apathy.
—Robert Lee

To use your leisure effectively, you need to have goals. We hear a lot about setting goals to maximize our efficiency on the job. Much of our orientation from early childhood is toward the planning of a career. A good portion of our school curriculum is aimed at preparing us to become members of the work force.

Our whole life is frequently built around finding the job or career that will prove challenging, stimulating, and worthwhile, as well as give us financial security. And once employed, our occupation can permeate every facet of our lives—the time we wake up, where we live and commute, who we meet and spend our time with, when we eat, how we dress, and even how we think and feel about ourselves.

Everything else in our lives becomes incidental to this primary goal in life. Yet, as we have seen, few if any jobs provide an abundance of opportunities for self-fulfillment and creativity. We have needs for personal growth, for gaining insights about ourselves and the changing world in which we live, for physical well-being, for psychological health, for improved interpersonal relationships, and for a chance to let our curiosity loose as when we were children. A job cannot satisfy all these needs. Even establishing financial security solely through our work turns out to be unrealistic.

This is not a call to quit work and become unemployed or go on welfare, as some people are doing[1] only to recognize what the workplace can and cannot offer. Some firms and positions are better than others in terms of working conditions, challenge, or monetary compensation. And a number of progressive firms are now equipped with

---

1. B. Lefkowitz, Breaktime *(New York: Hawthorn Books, 1979).*

By making a commitment in our leisure, we can
move toward the goals of our choice

athletic clubs and other facilities in an attempt to serve the psycho-logical and health needs of their employees.[2]

In contrast to the limitations imposed upon us in most work settings, however, leisure opens the door to infinite possibilities and opportunities. But good things will not just happen in our leisure with no commitment on our part. It is essential that we know what we want and have a plan for obtaining it.

Eight steps to leisure commitment and success

Step 1: Brainstorming for success through leisure

Begin by making a list of all your aspirations, hopes, and dreams. List these as quickly as possible without any evaluation. Take ten minutes and write down everything that comes to mind about what you would like to *do* or *have* or *be*. For example:

• take a cruise off the coast of Yugoslavia
• earn a better return on your investments
• be more relaxed and slimmer

At this stage, don't worry about cost or how unrealistic your goals might be. Let your imagination flow freely. Close your eyes and let yourself drift into fantasy. Imagine being completely removed from your present day-to-day routine, from work, and from any financial restrictions. Step outside of yourself and think about just having entered a fresh, new life with no external obligations or demands, and no internal insecurities or anxieties. You are completely free to carve out whatever you want from life. What will it be?

By clarifying your desires and dreams in this way, you can give direction to your life. When you know exactly what you want, decision-making becomes less confusing; you know what is relevant, what to eliminate from your life, and what to add.

The goals we set for ourselves in leisure, however, are not meant to be fixed or permanent. What we want is not a rigid, inflexible plan but one that is subject to revision as we grow and change. Nor are our

---

2. R. Young, *"Working out at Work, or How Corporations Intend to Trim the Fat,"* Next, *March/April, 1981, pp. 74-83.

Brainstorming for success

goals to be viewed strictly as end-products. Most of us are continually striving to get somewhere. But it is in *the process of moving toward our goals* that we discover happiness. Happiness is not found in arriving somewhere, but is a by-product of knowing what we want and progressing in that direction.

Many of us have become so used to others making decisions for us and telling us what we want—the media, commercials, parents, friends, employers, and lovers—that we don't really know who we are or what we like. If this is the case for you, begin by probing yourself to discover what kinds of things you enjoy most and find rewarding. The starting point for anything you do needs to be made out of the context of a clear free space. This is what leisure is all about. It is void of any pressures, obligations, others' demands, "ought-to's" and "should-do's." Play around with the objectives you have set down for yourself. Your gift of leisure is for you to do with as you like, in keeping with your own personal framework of values and wishes.

Step 2: Culling your list

After listing all the possibilities that flow into your mind, take a few minutes to evaluate each of them. Are any of your objectives inconsistent with each other? Perhaps you stated that you would like to spend less time commuting to your office in the city, but you also want to move to the mountains, even farther away from the office. Which is more important? What other alternatives might satisfy both desires? For example, you might get an apartment in the city close to work for weekdays and have a retreat in the mountains on weekends and for vacations. Or you could talk with your employer about flextime and working only three or four days per week.

One of my clients, George, wrote that he would like to be more relaxed and free of pressures; even on weekends he was anxious and uptight. He also wrote that he'd like to "beat his boss's ass off" at tennis. He explained how, every Saturday and Sunday, he was knocking himself out on the tennis courts with his boss, who was a much better player than he was. Tennis for George was neither fun nor relaxing; it was keeping him strung out. A Type-A on the job, this carried over into his leisure, and he played every game in a fiercely competitive spirit.

In looking over your desires, ask yourself if there are any conflicts or inconsistencies. What do you really want? Eliminate those that contradict other, more important goals.

Step 3: Getting specific

After you have culled your list, you may find that many of your desires are still a bit too general for you to set up a plan for their realization. At this point, you want to fill in the details. For example, suppose you listed that you want to travel. Narrow it down to specifics. Where? What countries and cities? Do you like rural or urban areas? What form of transportation do you prefer in order to reach your destination: Airplane, train, or ocean cruiser? Whom would you like to travel with? Do you prefer to travel alone, with a friend, or with a large group of people?

Perhaps you stated that you wanted to make sounder investments. What kind of investments—the stock market, real estate, commodities, antiques? What percentage of return do you want? What kinds of risk are you willing to take? Think it through until you have a clear notion of what's right for you and your particular situation.

Many people say that they would like to have more self-confidence. If this is one of your objectives, ask yourself exactly what "self-confidence" means to you. Being relaxed and assertive in a group setting? Being able to express yourself with the opposite sex? Not being intimidated by authority figures? In what kinds of situations do you lack self-confidence and with what types of people?

Fill in enough details until you can actually visualize each success-goal as a specific mental image. In a later chapter, you will see how you can turn these mental pictures into realities in your life.

Step 4: Determining your success categories

You will find that the desires you have listed fall into various categories. Group them together using the sample categories below as a guide:

Success category	Goal
Physical fitness	Jump rope for 10 minutes a minimum of 3 times per week
Relationships	Initiate 2 new contacts with a member of the opposite sex each week
Financial	Set up an investment program of stocks and bonds for an annual return of 30 percent

Emotional	Clear my head of work projects and relax after work
Vacation	Charter a sailboat to Baja California
Career	Stop working overtime
Educational	Enroll in a sculpture class at the university
Community-International	Volunteer Saturday mornings at a local futurist group to help establish better international relations

Grouping your desires and ambitions helps you to further crystallize them and gives you focus. You can create your own success categories if you like, but limit yourself to no more than eight. Don't be concerned if some of them overlap. Think about each category in relation to yourself, your interests, and your values. The categories may suggest additional needs or desires that you did not explore in the previous steps.

After you have grouped your success-goals, go back and choose your *five most important* ones.

Step 5: What is your degree of desire?

Realizing personal success through leisure involves deciding not only *what* you want, but *why* you want it. As a measure of your desire for each goal, you might ask yourself what you would be willing to give up in order to achieve it. If you do not have a strong desire for a particular goal, the first time something or someone comes along that interferes with your achieving it, you will drop it or be lax about doing it. If you want to stop working overtime but have not thought through the benefit to yourself of more spare time, the first time you get pressure from your employer to work late, your resistance will collapse.

As you begin to initiate changes in your life, keep in mind their value to you. Write them down, and keep the list someplace handy as a reminder. A strong commitment to your objectives will help pull you through inertia, bad times, and all the things that can go wrong to separate you from greater personal success.

Step 6: Using a Time-Reactor-Log as a change instigator

The Time-Reactor-Log (TRL) is a means to keep track of where your time is going and how you are reacting to the events of the day. Using the illustration on page 93 as a guide, take a sheet of paper or a pre-printed daily calendar page and, on the left-hand side, begin writing down exactly where your time has gone. Log this in about every two hours during the day and evening. On the right-hand side, under "Reactions," jot down briefly how you respond to the events of the day, that is, your thoughts and feelings.

Do this for at least three days, preferably a Saturday, a Sunday, and one weekday. In addition, on the back of the pages, put down what you believe to be any significant factors or events that seem to be either interfering with or aiding you in reaching your success-goals. Specifically, what seems to be causing those incomplete projects, your frustration, or your inability to relax? On the positive side, what appears to be boosting your self-confidence, keeping you energized and on track?

Doing this will help you to achieve the personal successes you have outlined. Using a TRL gives you an edge in three ways:

(1) It raises your awareness of the way you spend your time and how this relates to your goals and your enjoyment. It is one thing to *feel* that time is getting away from you, but quite another to *know*—to see it written down in black and white. Also, putting forth the effort to write it down will make you more conscious of the potential of all the hours you have available.

(2) You become a more objective observer of your behavior. Accurate observation of your reactions to the events in your life will help you to understand what forces are influencing you and their impact upon you. We all know that a lot of things are preventing us from realizing the kinds of successes we are capable of, but the TRL helps us zero in on specifics.

(3) With the TRL, you will begin to see the specific time-wasters that diminish your leisure time. The TRL will help make you more conscious of the kinds of things in your life that are related to any worries, anxieties, insecurities, or other self-defeating emotions. In addition, your TRL gives you a clearer picture of what you are doing right, and those factors (whether internal or external) that are contributing to your success.

In other words, through a TRL you can increase your awareness of what you are doing and the forces shaping your time and life. You

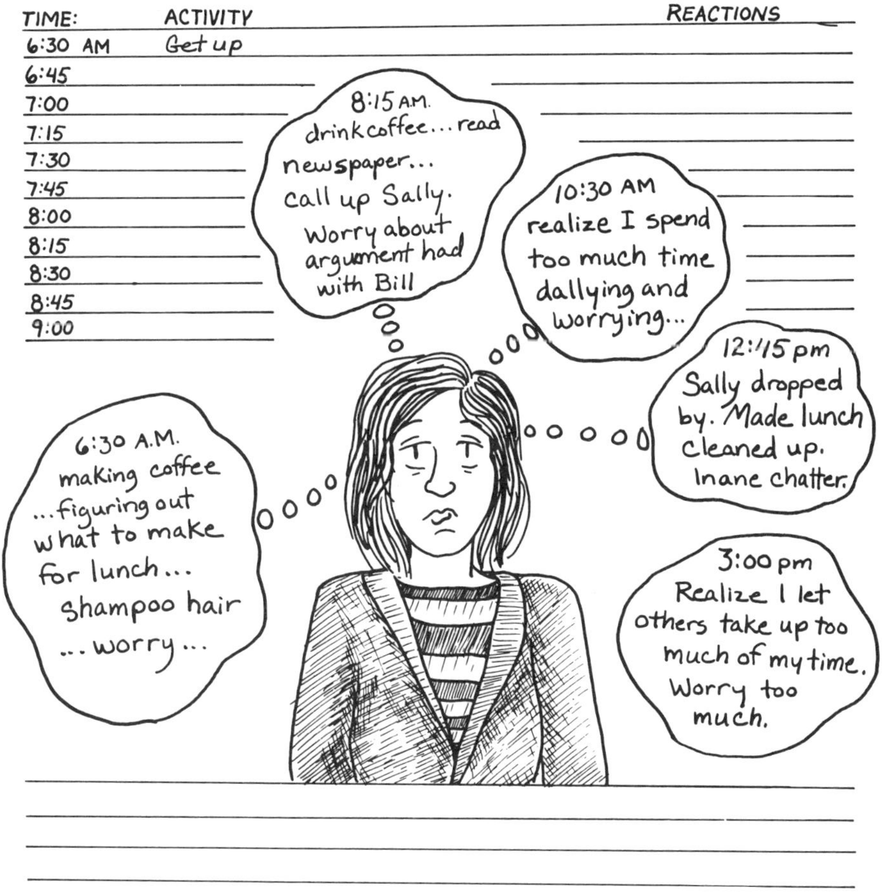

Using a Time-Reactor-Log can act as a change instigator

become more conscious of how you are spending your time, the habits you have gotten into, and how your habits inhibit or enhance your chances for success.

Using a TRL will then act as a change instigator. Once you have clearly understood what you are presently doing and what you could be doing, you are ready to begin closing the gap between the actual and the ideal.

Step 7: Matching up time spent and goal priorities

Reviewing your TRL, take a look at how your time spent corresponds with the goals and priorities you set out for yourself in the earlier steps. All too often the largest percentage of our time is spent on those things that are *least* important to us, while only a small amount of our time goes to our most vital concerns. Complete the Goals and Time Spent chart on p. 95. Write down your priorities as you listed them in Step 4 above, and record the amount of hours spent on each (actual and ideal). What changes need to be made?

Step 8: Setting a date for change

The final step in making a commitment to leisure success is to set a deadline. Some of your objectives will be short-term, such as those things you want to have happen today, next week, and next month. Others will be intermediate, to be achieved six months from now or next year. Still others will be long-term, to be achieved five or ten years from now. Put a *definite date* after each of your success-goals and then enter these in your calendar. (If you do not already have a time-planning calendar, make a note to yourself now to purchase one.)

Never set a deadline that you will be unable to keep. And never tell yourself you are going to do something that you may not presently be able to do. Start out small. If you have decided that thirty minutes of exercise each morning would be right for you, but you have not been exercising at all for the past two years, begin with only five minutes a day and gradually build up to thirty. Success builds on success. Even the small things on your list when done *as you have decided* (and that is the key) will give you confidence and help you to move on to your more important goals.

GOALS AND TIME SPENT

List of Goals	Time Spent (hours)	
	Actual	**Ideal**
1. _____	_____	_____
2. _____	_____	_____
3. _____	_____	_____
4. _____	_____	_____
5. _____	_____	_____
6. _____	_____	_____
7. _____	_____	_____
8. _____	_____	_____
9. _____	_____	_____
Total	_____	_____

How does your time spent correspond with your priorities?

Changes you can expect

Once you have made a commitment to success through leisure, you will begin to observe a number of incidental changes in your life. You will find that your emotional pattern is becoming more positive. Your face and posture will take on a more relaxed expression. You'll have a greater sense of humor and see more spontaneous laughter in yourself. Your curiosity and zest in living will also blossom. You will find that you have more of a genuine concern for others and are more tolerant. This in turn will result in more satisfying personal relationships. You will be free from boredom and less likely to find yourself "just killing time" or letting others kill time for you, because now time has become very special to you.

IV
STRATEGIES FOR LEISURE SUCCESS

A rational, scientific, and eclectic approach to leisure success is presented in this section. It draws on psychocybernetics, information processing theory, and Far Eastern philosophy. It is a direct, straightforward, no hocus-pocus approach that builds on the thought resources you have now and gives you the means for expanding your leisure potential and success in whatever areas you choose.

In order to bring about personal success through leisure quickly and effectively, it is necessary to work at both the conscious and preconscious levels of your mind. The conscious level is your normal waking state, the so-called beta level of consciousness where you make decisions and solve problems. At the conscious level occur activities such as defining, clarifying, and making a commitment to the kinds of personal successes you chose in the previous chapter. Once you know what you want, why you want it, and have made a commitment consistent with your values, interests, and personality needs, you are ready to maximize your efforts toward positive change in these areas.

Strategies for bringing about change are also active at the preconscious level. It is not enough simply to know what you want and have a conscious plan for obtaining it. Lifelong behavior patterns and habits turn out to be quite resistant to the best intentions and adamant to the strongest will. You also need to set your inner stage for success, to activate your inner resources so that new behaviors will become automatic and reflexive. In the following chapters, we will discuss both of these means and how they can work together for you.

7.
Scimode: A
Conscious Strategy
for Success

One does not stumble into success.
—Anonymous

Becoming . . . in time

One very powerful and effective general strategy at the conscious
level is *Scimode*. (The concept and theoretical basis for Scimode was
developed from my research in leisure and personality.) Scimode is a
dynamic, flexible, action-oriented means for resolving any leisure
ailments that are limiting you and your success, as well as any future
problems that may arise. Scimode has to do with *becoming . . . in
time*. It is becoming a scientist in your own field of experience in order
to better predict, control, and understand your time space. It is
becoming more objective, analytic, and "self" conscious in the sense
of learning to "stand over yourself" and accurately observe and
identify those factors and forces impinging on your time. The Time-
Reactor-Log (TRL) which we discussed in the last chapter is an
integral part of this process and will aid your progress here as you
keep track of your time and consciously observe how you are being
affected by the circumstances of your life.

Scimode is more than a strategy; it is an attitude, an orientation to
thinking and acting whereby you gain greater control over your time.
When we think about *control*, we may think about science, and
sometimes we think about manipulation on the negative side, or
understanding on the more positive side. Through Scimode, you will
be moving toward positive control, manipulation, and understanding
of your *own* use of time.

Becoming . . . in time means both "freedom from" and "freedom to."
It involves making those choices that will result in:

- *Freedom from* all those things invading your time and preventing you from achieving your objectives. These may be internal constraints, such as procrastination, anxiety, or apathy, as well as those external forces, such as others' demands, pressures, or environmental phenomena that are acting to limit your success.
- *Freedom to* recognize, create, and pursue those opportunities available to you. These may take the form of financial freedom and creating some spare time to maximize your investment resourcefulness. It may mean developing better personal relationships that are free from hostilities, misunderstandings, and frustration. Or it might be pursuing a sound physical fitness plan, having a higher energy level and enjoying overall well-being.

Science and Scimode

Often it seems as if events outside of ourselves are determining what happens to us and how we feel. We live in a world of startling inconsistencies, an information explosion, congestion, the nuclear threat, rampant inflation and economic recession. It is a world saddled with political chaos, organized crime, religious fanaticism, racial bigotry, and sexual violence. In such an irrational world, no wonder we find ourselves feeling insecure, anxious, worried, burned out, jittery, or nervous. Nor is it any wonder that we're prone to fights with our mate, frustration, hostility, and anger. And it is hardly surprising that we react by indulging in excesses: overeating, drinking, and smoking too much.

It is easy to place the blame outside ourselves, keep busy, and structure our time so as to avoid any uncomfortable reflection about a world over which we appear to have little control. But in spite of external events and conditions, we can take charge of our own habit patterns and feelings to insure more personal well-being and success. Through Scimode you discover how best to interfere—to take control of your time yourself. You learn what forces are acting on you and seem to be causing what you do not wish to happen. You then discover ways to manipulate these forces so that they begin working for you instead of against you.

In effect, you are taking on the role of the scientist, but not a scientist in some specialized field of knowledge, such as physics or chemistry. You "become a scientist" in your own field of experiences. You study what factors are associated with your frustrations, with losing time, or with realizing specific goals. You are then in a position to either eliminate or minimize those factors that are constricting your leisure and success, or to create more favorable consequences.

Like the scientist, you begin by accumulating data—data about yourself. Of course, you have been accumulating information about yourself for years, and just as the scientist turns to past bodies of knowledge to develop new hypotheses, you will begin your self-study with your past body of information about yourself. The more accurate the "links" or hypotheses you are able to generate from your own field of experience, the greater will be your freedom. Developing a reservoir of links gives you the power to take charge of your life so that you are no longer subject to chance and fate but become the creator of the circumstances in your life.

Scimode, then is a method that aids you in discovering more about the forces that shape your time. Fortunately, you do not need to know everything about the laws of your behavior in order to effect significant changes. Simply understanding a few simple but crucial principles is sufficient. Through Scimode you discover how both internal and external forces interact to shape your life and how you can channel and change them to create a time space more of your choosing.

Scimode is an umbrella under which all more specific strategies fall. It is what we all use to some degree, but mostly in an inconsistent, haphazard fashion. When you begin using Scimode consciously, you develop the habit of being more open, curious, and objective, and learn to take an experimental approach to living.

One reason why science and technology have gotten out of hand in the world today is because we haven't personalized them—i.e., made them a comfortable part of our own decision-making. *Scimode* comes from the terms "science" and "mode"; it is a scientific mode of thinking about ourselves in interaction with our environment. By becoming more objective in our thinking and learning to identify the relevant forces that determine the form of our existence, we gain the predictive power to allow our fondest dreams to unfold.

The goal here is not to become a scientist or psychologist in the sense of discovering "laws of behavior" applicable to everyone. One of the mistakes social scientists have made is patterning their formulas for predicting human behavior after those of the physical sciences. But each of us and the situations we find ourselves in are unique in so many respects that this is a foolhardy objective. As living, volitional entities we have a "feedback mechanism" that, as it becomes better understood, provides us with the means for changing our experiences and our world in accordance with our values and desires. What we need to do is to take the tools of science out of the lab and put them into our own lives. Only then can we gain a measure of control over our lives and, as a society, begin to evolve from an irrational to a rational world in time.

Two models to reject

Scimode is based on the assumption that we need not be greatly determined by biological or environmental factors. The "nature-nurture" issue has long been buried, with researchers today studying the interactive effects of our genetic make-up and external variables. Nevertheless, many among us still fall into one or the other camp. The "nature" group people continue to tell us that most everything is written in the genes and the best we can do is discover just what it is, accept it, and act accordingly. However, if you accept this deterministic position, where does it leave you? If you honestly believe that your biological make-up is responsible for the kind of person you are and the successes or failures you achieve, you are unlikely to play an active role in bringing about changes yourself.

The environmentalists, on the other hand, argue that it is not so much our genes but the events in our lives—our socialization, the rewards and punishments we receive, the elements—that determine who we are and what we achieve. Yet according to the "nurture" theorists, too, the individual is but a pawn in a game of forces over which she or he has little or no control. Many of the conclusions about human behavior drawn by both camps have been inferred from research with lower animals, such as rats and pigeons. But, in fact, the higher we move up the phylogenetic scale, from amoebas to primates, the *less* our behavior is determined by our genes and the *more* flexibility we have in directing our own fate.

Although the two positions above represent extremes and have been oversimplified, they still influence many of our beliefs and keep us from taking charge of our lives. In order for you to shape your own time, it is imperative that you abandon determinism and take the full responsibility yourself.

Becoming more "self" conscious

We all have at least two selves: an overself and the self of our experiences that we are caught up in. The overself is the pure scientist

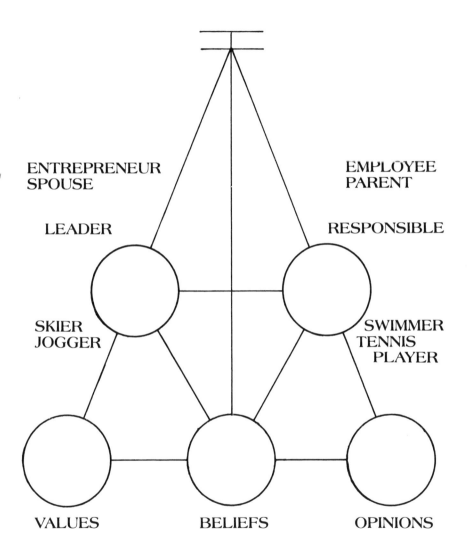

ENTREPRENEUR
SPOUSE

EMPLOYEE
PARENT

LEADER

RESPONSIBLE

SKIER
JOGGER

SWIMMER
TENNIS
PLAYER

VALUES   BELIEFS   OPINIONS

Standing over ourselves

of your mind; it is the part of you that can see clearly the phenomena of life "as is." There is no pretense, no ego at stake, and no fear of what this full, unhampered look at reality might bring. Another characteristic of your overself is its universal spirit and sense of freedom; it is not bound to or limited by any belief system, preconceived ideas, roles, labels, or other verbal handles that humans use in their daily business.

In becoming more "self" conscious, not in the sense of embarrassment but in "standing over yourself," over your beliefs, values, opinions, and past experiences, you are in a position to move toward greater predictive power. Our ego is tied up in these elements of ourselves and in the roles that we play (mother, father, wife, husband, provider, homemaker, manager, lover, leader, and so on). By "standing over yourself," i.e., by transcending your particular set of values, beliefs, and experiences, you are able to become a more objective observer of your behavior and of the factors that influence you. Only by separating ourselves from our beliefs and biases can we accurately take note of the data which experience brings to us.

Sometimes our ego intrudes, and we do not see things as clearly as we otherwise might. When confronted with ideas or points of view that are in opposition to our own, we may back away or get defensive. In the face of criticism or attacks on our pet ideas, long-held opinions and cherished beliefs, we often become overly emotional and protective, and may even feel a sense of threat to our very existence. This clouds our thinking, jeopardizes our well-being, and prevents us from learning and taking effective action. You need to recognize that you are much more than the roles you play, the positions you occupy, and the beliefs and opinions which you presently hold.

In "standing over yourself" you are temporarily letting go—releasing—all those mental constructs that are bound to the self of your experiences; you are then able to relate to your past body of information free of any insecurities, threats, or emotions that might get in the way.

Human self-consciousness was born out of leisure and is still but a flicker in our total existence. We are barely becoming aware of ourselves, how we react and interact with the events in our lives and how our thinking can improve or damage the quality of life. We are "on top of ourselves" only momentarily, and then topple to the level of pure experience. Operating within our experiences, we flow with the life stream in joy, in anguish, in love, or in hate. Only when we step into our overself are we able to gain perspective, see events as they really are, and reprogram ourselves for change.

By stepping into our overself, we can gain
perspective and reprogram for change

Getting away from fuzzy labels: identifying links

We usually label our behavior broadly. We say we cannot do the things we would really like to do because we lack "will power," we have too many "interruptions," and we "procrastinate." But what we need is to be specific. What do we mean by "procrastination" or "interruptions"? What specifically is happening and what are the consequences? Once you have identified the particular links, you are on the way to making the modifications for the outcome you want.

Let's say your TRL shows that "interruptions" are eating up your time and resulting in annoyance and frustration. You have been trying to get a new project started, prepare for an important meeting, finish writing a manuscript, or perhaps simply relax and read a good book. Somehow things just keep interfering with these objectives.

"What can I do?" you ask. "All I had today was one interruption after another." But attaching labels to the circumstances in our lives only blurs the actual conditions. Instead of simply attributing your lack of progress to "interruptions," zero in on the specifics. *What kind* of interruptions? Noise, such as traffic, laughter, clinking dishes, ringing telephones, or people chattering? Unexpected visitors? Kids asking questions? *When* do the interruptions occur? At what time of day—morning, afternoon, or evening? On what day of the week are they most likely to occur—Monday, Friday, Saturday? *Where* are they most likely to occur? *How often? How intense* are they? Only after you have zeroed in on precisely *how* your time is disappearing are you in a position to make changes for a more desirable outcome.

Although this may sound tedious, once the Scimode habit is established, it will quickly become second nature. For example, suppose the telephone is a big time-waster for you, as it is for many people. Your telephone can waste your time several ways: calls may come at inopportune times; you may spend unnecessary amounts of time talking or listening; or you may have inefficient means of making calls, returning calls, and handling waiting time. But each of these can be put under your control. Arrange to answer calls when you're taking a break from that important project. Respond to a ringing phone only when it makes sense and fits into your life style. I have seen people answer a phone right in the middle of dinner, talk for fifteen minutes while their dinner gets cold, and then spend the rest of the dinner complaining about it. People get out of the shower, soapy and wet, to answer a phone call that turns out to be someone selling

Ask yourself, "What are the links?"

magazine subscriptions or a new roof. We're so conditioned, we even grab the phone when we're about to have a sexual climax!

Many alternatives are available. Answering machines are relatively inexpensive. If you do not like the impersonality of a machine, answering services can be hired for as little as twenty dollars a month. At the office, you can perhaps have your secretary or assistant screen your calls. How you structure the change will depend on you and your unique set of circumstances. The important point is to (1) identify *exactly* what is interfering with your objectives and well-being, i.e., what are the links? and (2) recognize that it is not inevitable—you can intervene to break the link and obtain more satisfactory results.

Let's look at another example. You are trying to complete a project and making no progress. This time, there are no interruptions. But you feel sluggish, lack pep and energy, and cannot seem to get yourself going. Pin it down to specifics. What are the links? *When* do you lack pep and energy? Mornings, afternoons, or evenings? *Where* do you feel the most enervated? In the office or at home? Indoors or outdoors? In a metropolitan area or in a rural area? When you are alone or surrounded by people? *What* has happened immediately preceding your listlessness? Did you eat a heavy lunch, have a cocktail or two? Did you have an argument with a friend or lover? Or did you perhaps just *recall* an unhappy or frustrating incident in your life? What kind of self-talk are you feeding yourself? The answers to these specific questions will help you plan effective change.

I was having lunch one day with a young advertising executive who had been assigned to a big account and was feeling the pressure of an approaching deadline. "I just can't seem to get into it," he told me. "I wake up in the morning and think, 'Oh, that awful project, and only four days left!' "

What was this executive's problem? Ever since his assignment eight months before, he apparently had been telling himself, "What a dud this job is," "The company is all screwed up," and "They're not going to be satisfied with anything that I do." With that kind of continuous self-talk, he was not only failing to get the job done, but jeopardizing his health by fretting about it. For him, the crucial link was his own self-defeating internal chatter.

Links can be positive as well as negative. Look closely at when you're functioning at your best. One day, lo and behold, you find yourself feeling clear-headed, bubbling with energy, able to concentrate and think creatively, and motivated to complete the task at hand. What are the links? Did you sleep more soundly than usual the night before? Have you been getting more physical exercise? Has turning down the furnace made you more alert? Have you been enjoying more or better sex? Has your self-talk been more success-oriented?

Perhaps you can associate particular times of day or night with the way you feel. Many of us have a peak time when we're more alert, clear-minded, and creative. It can be early morning, afternoon, or even the middle of the night. One of my clients, the mother of two young daughters, explained to me that she had a burning desire to write a book of poetry about some of her travel experiences, but, like many of us, was unable to see how she could schedule it into her busy days. Adela worked full-time, and had tried to jot down some material evenings after work, but felt guilty about taking precious time away from her children. By the time they were in bed and she had finished her household chores, she was too drained to write anything but the tritest lines. On weekends, she took accelerated university classes toward a master's degree, so that time was also out.

In going over her TRL, we discovered the link. It seems she was constantly waking up in the middle of the night and was unable to go back to sleep. My first inclination was to give her some strategies for quickly falling back to sleep. As we probed further, however, she told me, "You know, when I wake up at night, my mind really seems to be sharp. All these ideas for my poetry pop into my head—some of them quite good, I think—but, by morning, I've usually forgotten them."

Adela's peak time turned out to be between two and four A.M. She found that she could get up during those hours, write her poetry, promptly fall back to sleep, and wake up in the morning feeling better than ever. She never missed the two hours' sleep.

Mentally run through the events in your life and try to pinpoint those positive links in your life. Put yourself under surveillance for a few days. What kinds of habits have you gotten into? What are you doing or not doing that is related to anxiety, boredom, frustration, or excesses in your life? What factors precipitate those times when you are at your best, enjoying life most, and getting on with your goals? What are the environmental links and what are the thought links? Once you begin to identify how A is causing B and C is producing D, you are on the way to extra hours and happier hours.

Our black space and how it limits our success

The illustration below shows how various forces act on us and can result in consequences that we do not want. The "black space" represents that part of your self that is void of any awareness or conscious control. The white area shows the sliver of your potentially conscious self actively intervening to produce the outcomes you would like. This model holds true for most of us; we have only minimal control over our lives. However, this need not be the case.

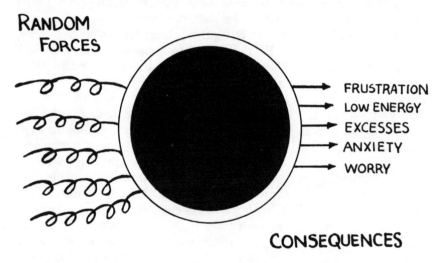

RANDOM
FORCES

FRUSTRATION
LOW ENERGY
EXCESSES
ANXIETY
WORRY

CONSEQUENCES

Our black space and how it acts to limit our success

In order to expand your potential control—the white area in the diagram—you need to become aware of the forces linked with the ways you act and feel. Whenever you get a result you do not want, attempt to connect it back to the eliciting event.

"But," you may protest, "there are so many forces that shape our lives, how can I ever begin to identify all of them?" The happy truth is that you do not need to know *all* of the variables affecting your time; all you need to be aware of are the key factors. Important changes, in fact, leaps and bounds in your progress toward success, can become a reality *by way of only a few significant and accurate observations.*

What goes on inside the black space is crucial. With no awareness or conscious intervention on your part, the forces about us slip through to mold and shape our lives at whim. If we have not grasped the links in our life, they are free to act upon us at will, leaving us subject to forces we are minimally prepared to deal with.

Reversing the process: giving yourself control

As the illustration on page 112 depicts, we can expand our awareness and our area of conscious control to minimize the effects of random forces upon us. We can intervene to negate the effect of unwanted links in our lives and produce the kinds of results we desire.

As you learn to become a more precise observer, generate new links, and test them out in experience to check their validity, you build up a repertoire of facts rather than fictions. From this base, your predictions and expectations become more in tune with reality. Using Scimode, you can open up your time to new success and prosperity by accurately identifying and then taking charge of the forces related to the ends you desire.

No one knows you better than you do. Authorities or so-called experts know very little—especially about you. It's you who know best who you are and what you are capable of doing. Often, however, we shortchange ourselves because of the opinions of others. You are always the final authority in your life. Through Scimode, you learn how to sift through the jumble of information and forces surrounding you to make the kinds of decisions that are right for your unique situation.

Links to success

Links are to the lay person what hypotheses are to the scientist. They are statements of the factors that result in probable consequences. If the barometric pressure is at 80, there is a high chance of rain. With knowledge of this association, we carry an umbrella to keep from getting wet. If we know that robberies are prevalent in our neighborhood, we keep our doors locked to safeguard our property. By having accurate links, we can *prepare* ourselves for what we cannot control, *prevent* unwanted results, *modify* a situation so that the association no longer holds, or *create the conditions* for what we do want. We cannot always prevent a particular event from occurring, but, by being

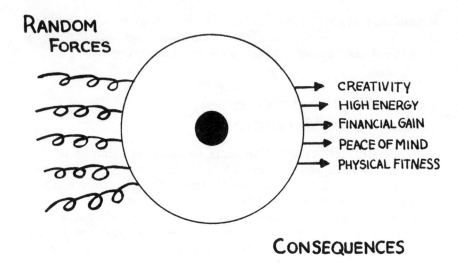

RANDOM FORCES

CREATIVITY
HIGH ENERGY
FINANCIAL GAIN
PEACE OF MIND
PHYSICAL FITNESS

CONSEQUENCES

Reversing the process: giving yourself control

aware of key factors in our lives and their probable effects, we can intervene to reduce their negative impact.

Here are some examples. If you have tried to stop smoking six times only to begin again, each time feeling rotten and guilty about your lack of will power, you can right now give yourself permission to smoke and enjoy it until you discover the relevant link that will enable you to permanently quit. In this way, although you have not yet learned how to prevent an unwanted behavior, you have intervened to reduce its negative psychological consequences.

If you discover that a particular song or piece of music enhances your peace of mind and restores your energy, you can keep a cassette handy to create this condition within yourself at the times you choose.

If you have noted that being around highly motivated, success-oriented people stimulates your own motivation, you can take steps to increase your contacts of this kind. As obvious as these examples may seem, most of us are careless observers in our personal lives and fail to consciously intervene on our own behalf.

The greater the number of accurate links in your life, the greater will be your freedom and success. We use a scientific approach in research to better predict, control, and understand the world; we use it in business to increase the profit margin; we use it in the military to outwit our foes; *but in our personal lives—that most vital area—we* have neglected it almost totally. Only as we begin to use Scimode systematically in our day-to-day affairs, when it becomes a habitual way of thinking, will we break free from the external pressures, demands, and obligations that bind us and the debilitating forces of our inner space.

Scimode and the people in your life

Practically everything in our lives involves others either directly or indirectly. Even when we are alone, our thoughts, feelings, and decisions revolve around the people in our lives. From the day we are born we interact with others—siblings, parents, friends, colleagues, relatives, and strangers. Yet for all our exposure to people, we often act irrationally, immaturely and unrealistically in our social lives. We get upset without warrant. We are insensitive and contribute to others' pain. We search for love and joy in our lives while acting in ways that preclude any possibility of finding it. We lash out angrily at one another, jeopardizing our health and our sanity.

Why all this nonsense? Much of our insanity here has to do with living in a world of fiction rather than fact. We have not acquired the habit of observing others from a Scimode orientation. We lump people into convenient, stereotyped categories: "lazy, rude, selfish, egotistical, ruthless . . ." But, as we have seen, labels do not explain behavior; they only prevent us from discovering the links that would help us to have more realistic expectations. Only by carefully noting the explicit differences among people and their effects on us can we accurately predict their behavior and our own and move toward more sensitive interactions. Each person is an extraordinary entity different in many respects from everyone else. It is our ability to detect the differences and how they affect us that will result in the outcomes we would like.

You will not try to change the people you associate with. That would be the most difficult way to achieve what you want. What you need is to know where the other person is coming from and act on that basis. You gain control not by trying to directly control the other person's nature but by recognizing what kind of person he is and what can be expected from him. This is done by careful observation of his reactions. Your aim is simply to be able to *predict* those reactions. Once you can accurately predict another's responses, you are in control even if that person cannot be changed.

For example, if you know someone is going to lash out at you unfairly and unjustly at regular intervals, instead of concentrating on what a beast he is, try this: Using Scimode, calmly make a mental note of what is happening. (1) He is lashing out at you. (2) You are becoming hurt, angry, and upset. (3) The angrier you get, the worse he becomes. Don't attempt to psychoanalyze the other's behavior. Simply state as objectively as possible exactly what is happening.

Next, decide what you want. What consequences would you like to have? Perhaps you would prefer not to be hurt, angry, and upset. Even if you cannot change the other person's behavior, you always have a choice about how you are going to react. You are not a helpless, passive recipient of the forces in your life; you have control over your thought system, and can decide on the reaction best for you. And the more you exercise that right, the easier it will become, and the freer you will be.

You can make up your mind, then, to feel however you choose regardless of the circumstances in your life. When you begin to feel hurt, angry, or upset, ask yourself what good it is doing you. Do you want to be a martyr? If not, make a decision about what you really want and then follow through with Scimode. This means trying out different reactions and checking the consequences. Respond to another's anger with warmth and love. What happens? Respond by leaving the room. Hit back. Laugh. Make funny faces. Experiment with the different possibilities until you get the results you want.

In experimenting with different response options, it is not always necessary or even advisable to try everything out in experience. By building up a repertoire of accurate links, you can often predict consequences by mental testing. You may know perfectly well what will happen if you laugh or chide someone in an angry, hostile mood. But in other cases, you will not know because you have trucked along with the same old dysfunctional pattern of responses for so long.

With a storehouse of accurate links, your expectations are set straight. When your expectations are in keeping with what is actually happening, you can run through all the possible alternative reactions and decide on those that are most likely to give you the results you want.

Using Scimode to become more successful, then, depends on:
(1) The accuracy of your observations of the people and situations in which you find yourself;
(2) The number of links you have established;
(3) Recognizing that psychological links may change and need to be modified as we obtain new information; and
(4) Practice in testing out your links.

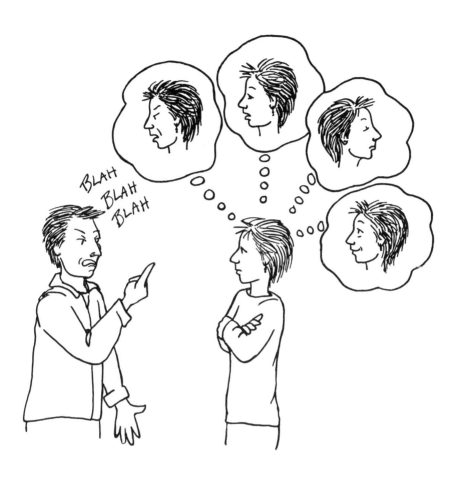

Response options

The bottom line is: Does it work? Does the association still hold? Does what you expected happen? If not, then it's time to revise your link. Go back to your observations; what did you overlook? Were you able to stand over yourself and survey the situation without any ego-shielding? *No ego is involved* when you are using Scimode correctly.

Following through with Scimode

Scimode is not developed overnight. It is a mental tool, a thought resource, that is cultivated with the right kind of practice. When you learn a new physical activity such as yoga, your muscles will resist your efforts at first. You may be able to stretch only a little toward the final desired position. But every time you do it, you come closer and closer to success. Practiced regularly and correctly, the exercise will soon feel right and be effortless. Your thought resources are the same. If Scimode has not been used, it may feel strange or unnatural initially. But after a while, it will become as automatic as combing your hair in the morning.

With Scimode, you will find your days more interesting, more of a challenge and exciting. There is no time to be bored or depressed because of the active role you play. Life is faced with confident expectation rather than fear or worry. When something goes wrong (i.e., your links do not turn out as you expected), you do not throw up your hands in despair and exclaim, "How could this happen?" You know how to reverse the process and create the outcome you want.

Scimode represents a new technology of thinking within our personal world of experience. It is a mode of thought that immediately "ups" the quality of life and provides a positive means for dealing with the uncertainties of today's world.

I am often asked, "Why have we taken so long to develop and use more adequate modes of thought?" One reason is that we have looked outside ourselves for the solutions to our problems. We have become dependent on the specialists in human nature to explain the laws and principles of behavior to us. *But there are no absolute or permanent laws of human behavior.* We are an open system with information continuously flowing in and out. And we use strategies to integrate, organize, and act on this information. Predictability and freedom in our personal life will come not from experts, but from our own observations and tools of thought.

This is not to say that the experts in human behavior are not of value to us. Their input can be quite helpful in formulating your links to success. But as a biologically and experientially unique entity, the missing link is always to be found through your own special processing.

Another reason for our tardiness in making progress in our interpersonal relations is that many of us do not realize the full impact of a new technology of thinking. We do not recognize how good life can be with this new thought resource. We have gotten used to our present style of living. We are getting by. Things are not that bad. But future generations will no doubt be astounded by the way we slop along in our personal and social relationships. To date, our personal affairs have been left mostly up to chance. By becoming scientists in our own field of experiences we can move toward a world and a life that is not just okay or not bad, but truly worthy of our time.

8.
Preconscious Strategies for Success

Only those who take leisurely what the people of the world are busy about can be busy about what the people of the world take leisurely.
—Chang Ch'ao

As vital as Scimode can be in our lives, we need to go a step further and set the *inner* stage for success as well. To bring about changes quickly, effectively, and painlessly, it is necessary to go beneath the surface and tap your inner resources. You can do this by displacing and weakening the old structures—all the myths, misconceptions, and dysfunctional habit patterns that are resisting your conscious efforts toward success. These are then replaced with information and mental images appropriate to your goals and desires.

This chapter will let you play your way into creating change. Within the framework of leisure, you need not trudge seriously and wearily toward some distant goal. You can enjoy yourself along the way, for the process whereby you realize your goals and potential is exciting and stimulating. During this process you will also make new discoveries about yourself. You may become aware of some new goals you had not thought about previously, or discard some of your earlier objectives. Some of the material goals you set out for yourself may become less important to you. But that is always your choice.

Dislodging the old dysfunctional patterns by constructing new success ideas and images involves three stages: (1) Putting yourself into *a heightened state of relaxation* where you are highly susceptible to suggestion; (2) *Plugging in selective information;* and (3) *Using mental imagery to maximize your success.*

Stage One: A heightened state of relaxation

In this age of stress and distress, many organizations and self-help books offer instructions on how to relax in order to relieve anxiety and tension. It feels good to be able to relax and let go of the tensions of the day. Here, however, we are not viewing relaxation as an end in itself. A heightened state of relaxation is a *means* by which you can reach into the innermost realms of your mind and make suggestions that will be accepted without question. This is known as your *alpha state*. Unlike your normal *beta state* of consciousness, you will get no arguments, no rationalizations, and no backtalk.

Let's say you have made a resolution to improve your physical fitness program. As one part of this, you decide to get up earlier to jog for twenty minutes every morning. You believe that you should be able to handle this easily enough (and of course you can), but the first morning the alarm goes off earlier you have a real struggle with yourself. You give yourself a dozen reasons why you should stay in bed: You got to bed late the night before. If you don't get your proper rest, you won't do well at an important meeting you have today. It feels colder than usual. It isn't even daylight yet. How important is jogging, anyway? There is a lot of controversy about the benefits of jogging. Conditions really aren't ideal to begin jogging right now. Maybe you'll have time before dinner this evening. The excuses go on and on. You assure yourself that you will either jog later today or go to bed earlier tonight and begin tomorrow. With that thought, you reset the alarm and drift back to sleep.

Or perhaps after a lot of back and forth self-talk you finally manage to sell yourself on the idea of dragging yourself out of bed and going out into the cold to jog. In either case it's uphill all the way.

Until getting out of bed earlier to jog becomes a routine part of your morning, it will continue to be a struggle *unless you go beneath the surface of your conscious will*. By putting yourself into a heightened state of relaxation where you are very susceptible to suggestion and plugging in a strong desire to get up early and jog, you can short-circuit all the arguments and rationalizations. Getting up then becomes an automatic response. The alarm goes off, you reach over to shut it off, and easily climb out of bed. There are no *if's, and's,* or *but's* about it.

This method can be used no matter what your objectives. Have you ever had writer's block? The internal struggle that keeps you away from the typewriter is bitter and frustrating. It drains your creative energies. And the longer you stay away from your manuscript, the harder the struggle and the worse you feel. Attempting to diet, quit smoking, or stop drinking excessively presents the same problem. Simply making a decision and trying to exert your will power is not successful for most people. Nor, as we discussed earlier, is it a matter of mustering up a stronger will. If you have been trying unsuccessfully to change your life, rest assured that it has nothing to do with being weak-willed. It has to do with the procedures you are using to bring about change. When you bypass your conscious mind and let your inner self know positively and definitely that you mean business about getting something, you will get it.

Too good to be true?

If it is all that easy, you may ask, why don't more people follow the preconscious route to change? Several reasons come to mind. As we stated earlier, most of us are fairly contented with life, and do not recognize the value and benefits of positive change. We have false beliefs about how difficult it might be to change. We think that for something to be valuable it has to be hard work.

Certainly there are many people who *wish* to improve. During their leisure time they read all the self-help books and attend every new seminar that comes along. They try Rolfing, Somatic Platonism, Transactional Analysis, Bioenergetics, Life Springs, I Can, Mandra Sex, Actualizations, Reichian Gestalt, Feldenkrais, Focusing, Neuro-Linguistic Programming, est, ad infinitum. Rather than becoming enlightened, however, they only become more confused.

The truth is, no one can give you anything that will produce any lasting changes *without your help. You* are the deciding factor in your life. We are far too skeptical of our own powers for creating positive change. I hope to convince you here to continue to be skeptical of others, but put more trust in *yourself* and your own powers.

Means of relaxation

Arriving at a heightened state of relaxation where you are more susceptible to suggestion can be achieved in a variety of ways. Some of the means that you might consider are yoga, massage, a jacuzzi or hot tub, sauna, mineral baths, and mud baths. More active forms of exercise, such as jogging, swimming, or dancing (especially aerobic), can also bring about a deep relaxation state. (Hypnosis, body work, and breathing exercises are other means for inducing relaxation and increasing your sensitivity to suggestion.)

Happy hour mud bath

You might think about the procedures that have been used by military groups and prison authorities for rendering their captives more susceptible to suggestion, commonly known as brainwashing. These means generally involve some form of deprivation, such as food deprivation, sleep deprivation, sensory deprivation (e.g., isolation), and not permitting captives to attend to bodily functions such as going to the bathroom. Many of these are used today in the name of human growth by groups whose members pay a fee of anywhere from $300 to $3,500 and willingly allow themselves to become captives. All forms of deprivation are likely to increase the person's vulnerability to authoritarian control and suggestion.

The major difference between these groups and the recommendations presented here is that someone else is controlling the situation instead of you. Thus, for you to consciously *choose* fasting or self-hypnosis as a means of programming in the kinds of changes *you* desire is a far cry from being at the mercy of someone else (whether that person is deemed benevolent or not).

Many of my clients have found a combination of deep breathing exercises, progressive muscle relaxation, and self-hypnosis to work well for them. We'll examine this method closely below.

Self-hypnosis

Many myths about hypnosis have evolved among the lay public, mostly because of the way it has been misused by entertainers and those who do not always have others' best interests in mind. Used properly, hypnosis is completely safe. With self-hypnosis, you do not lose control and are always fully in charge. What you are doing is going to your alpha level—an altered state of consciousness where you are deeply relaxed but still fully aware.

The alpha state is usually produced by a repetition of stimuli; for example, repeating the same statements over and over in a monotonous tone or chanting. In this state, suggestions become more effective than usual. You are able to screen out any distractions, internal or external, and focus only on what is being suggested.

When you go to "your level," as we'll call it, you will be suggesting to yourself those things you want to happen in your life, such as being better organized, developing the personal qualities you want in yourself, or achieving greater financial success.

Is gullibility associated with hypnotic susceptibility? Gullibility is not involved, but trust is. People who are more trusting can more easily be hypnotized. This is, perhaps, why children in general are more susceptible than adults. Also, persons who are more curious, adventurous, and imaginative can more readily be hypnotized than those who are overly cautious, rigid, and fearful.[1] Almost everyone, however, can attain a light state of hypnosis, and with some practice a medium to deep state can be induced.

Induction time (i.e., the time required to reach your level) varies among individuals from almost nothing to a few hours. Under the right conditions, light states can usually be reached in eight to ten minutes, and faster with practice.

The chief advantages of self-hypnosis are its easy accessibility under almost all situations and the speed with which it can bring about changes in your life. It is far less time-consuming and costly than many other procedures for change. And, most important, used in conjunction with other methods, it is extraordinarily effective in ridding oneself of unwanted emotional patterns (fears, insecurities), in producing new motivations and moods, and in eliminating dead time brought about by bad habits (drinking excessively, chain smoking, or incessant snacking).

Easing into hypnosis

Begin by getting into a comfortable position. You can be sitting or lying down, whichever is most convenient at the time. Now use progressive muscle relaxation to drain the tension from your body. Systematically tense up each muscle group in your body, hold it for a few seconds, and then let go and feel your muscles relax. If you have time, spend about fifteen minutes on this; if not, five to seven minutes is adequate. Next, take several deep breaths. Inhale slowly and deeply through your nose, filling first your stomach, then your chest. Hold it to the count of three; then exhale slowly through your mouth. Let your eyes close and relax. If you are sitting in a chair, let your head drop gently forward.

Now begin the process of induction by repeating a series of statements to yourself, out loud if possible. There are dozens of ways to do this. Here is one example:

"I am feeling comfortable and relaxed, thinking of nothing, nothing but the sound of my voice; my eyes are closed and I am feeling

---

1. *P. G. Zimbardo and F. L. Ruch,* Psychology and Life *(Glenview, IL: Scott, Foresman & Co., 1977), pp. 310-318. E. R. Hilgard,* Personality and Hypnosis: A Study of Imaginative Involvement *(Chicago: University of Chicago Press, 1970).*

Easing into hypnosis

comfortable and relaxed; the muscles in my face, my neck, my shoulders are relaxed, relaxed, and I am feeling comfortable and relaxed; my arms, my legs, my stomach, my whole body feels more and more relaxed; all the muscles of my body are comfortable and relaxed. I am thinking of nothing, nothing but the sound of my voice, concentrating only on my voice, thinking of nothing, absolutely nothing, feeling completely at peace and relaxed. I am breathing regularly and deeply, regularly and deeply, feeling more and more relaxed. Outside noises do not distract me, I am thinking of nothing, nothing but the sound of my voice, and I am going into a deep sound sleep, a deep sound sleep; relaxed and comfortable, relaxed and comfortable, always in control, but letting go, relax . . . relax . . . and I am going into a deep, deep sleep, a sleep where I will be fully aware, but totally relaxed, deeper and deeper . . . sleep . . . sleep . . . sleep. Counting from one to ten my sleep will get even deeper . . . deeper . . . one . . . deeper, still deeper . . . two . . . feeling relaxed, totally relaxed . . . three . . . deeper and deeper . . . four . . . still deeper, breathing regularly and deeply, regularly and deeply, my sleep is getting deeper and deeper . . . five . . . and I am in a deep sound sleep, feeling wonderfully relaxed, a deep sound sleep," and so on.

Spend about twelve to twenty minutes on induction initially. Later, you will be able to speed up the process. Before awakening, suggest to yourself that next time you will enter into an even deeper state. Also suggest to yourself that at no time will you lapse into a hypnotic state except by choice, nor will any person be able to hypnotize you against your will.

When you are ready to awaken, dehypnotize yourself as follows:

"I am beginning to awaken. In a minute I will awaken and feel completely refreshed and alert, completely refreshed and alert. I am beginning to awaken . . . my sleep is getting lighter, much lighter, and I am starting to awaken. Counting backwards from ten to one, my sleep is getting lighter and lighter, and at the count of one, I will be wide awake, wide awake, feeling wonderful, refreshed, and alert . . . ten . . . starting to awaken . . . nine . . . eight . . . one . . . I am now completely awake."

Many excellent books on self-hypnosis are available. I have listed a few of these in the Resource Directory.

An even easier way to enter into hypnosis is to make your own cassette tape and listen to it when you first wake up, when you have a break at the office, and before drifting off to sleep at night. Or you can purchase hypnosis cassettes on virtually everything, from improving your tennis game to attracting love, from becoming motivated for jogging to increasing your sexual prowess, from achieving financial independence to becoming more creative. See the Resource Directory for a list of some of these.

Stage Two: Plugging in selective information

After you have reached a heightened state of relaxation where you are highly susceptible to suggestion, the next step is to program in the kinds of things you want to happen in your life.

Go back to your list of desired successes. What personal characteristics have you set down for yourself? What kinds of relationships are important in your life? What financial goals have you outlined? What are your health and physical fitness requirements? Write these down in the form of self-affirmations. Use the examples below to stimulate your thought:

- I am an enthusiastic, energetic person.
- I organize my time well and do not waste time.
- Each morning when I awake, I feel fresh, alert, and excited about a new day.
- I am mentally alert and decisive and have good judgment at all times.
- I plan my time well.
- I am working less and enjoying life more.
- I complete projects that are important to me.
- I make time for those activities that are important to me.
- I am moving toward prosperity and success.
- I am jogging three miles a day.
- I eat those foods that are good for me.
- I eat (drink, smoke) lightly only.
- I am task-oriented and can easily handle whatever problems arise.
- I genuinely care about others and am a loving person.
- I can communicate my thoughts and feelings easily to others.
- Each day is a new adventure, exciting and challenging.
- Each day I am progressing toward my goals and objectives.
- I am a confident, independent, and self-sufficient person.
- I accept myself as I am now and do not require others' approval for high self-esteem.
- I feel relaxed and comfortable in all situations.
- I am a capable, competent person.

- I find it easy to do the things I want to do.
- Each day that I follow these procedures for my improvement, I move closer to personal success.
- I feel good about myself even though I am not perfect.
- I have established the Scimode habit and am a keen observer in my day-to-day affairs.

Use the list above only as a guide; tailor the affirmations to suit your specific needs and desires. Notice that they are stated in the first person and include both specific and general ideas.

How to program yourself for success

The following eight suggestions will get you started and keep you progressing in the right direction.

1. Decide on which category of success you want to begin with. Review Chapter Six and see where your priorities lie. For example, your list may look something like this:

        (A)   Physical Fitness/Health
        (B)   Relationships
        (C)   Financial Success
        (D)   Emotional Goals

The category of success that you elect to begin with will depend on what you determine to be most vital in your life right now. Give careful thought to this, and *reach a decision now.* Make up your mind that *this* is what you want and that you are going to follow through on it. No program, no matter how excellent, is going to work for you until you have *definitely decided* that this is what you want for yourself.

2. Take on only one category at a time. For any one session, plug in affirmations for either Physical Fitness or Financial Success, for example, but not both. Choose three to five affirmations appropriate to that category to incorporate in your thinking each session. If you have decided on Physical Fitness/Health, for example, you may have affirmations such as the following:

- I am exercising fifteen minutes each morning when I arise.
- I enjoy exercising and look forward to arising each morning.
- I eat only those foods that are nourishing and good for me.
- My body feels light and supple.

By taking on only one category at a time, you keep yourself focused in a single direction. Your mind becomes saturated and obsessed with the task at hand and goes all out for you. If you try to do several changes at the same time, you spread yourself too thin, and your preconscious becomes confused and not nearly as effective.

3. *During programming, always state your affirmations in positive terms.* Instead of saying, "I am no longer going to be an obese slouch and gorge myself with food," say "I am slim and eat only those foods that are good for me." Likewise, do not say, "I am going to stop being anxious, nervous, and depressed." Say, "I am confident, relaxed, and energetic." When you are in a hyper-suggestible state, you do not want even a hint of anything negative to enter your mind. Your concentration always needs to be on positive changes.

4. *Make statements in the present tense.* Do not say, "I *am going* to be successful and prosperous," say, "I *am* successful and prosperous." The changes in your life are beginning to take place *now*—not in some distant mañana. State your affirmations and begin thinking in the present moment; substitute "I am" for "I will be."

5. *When at your level, make your statements with as much feeling and conviction as you can. Pretend* that you already are in possession of your goals. *Act as if* you already had the desired success. *Assume the feeling* that would be yours if you did. At first, when you begin verbalizing your affirmations, you may find that counter-thoughts come back at you. "What? Who are you kidding? Me, a size 7? Me, earning $100,000 a year? What a joke!" However, if you persist and keep your mind made up that it *is* happening, it will.

One word of caution here. Don't plug in something so far-fetched that you cannot begin to conceive of yourself being it or having it. However, don't worry too much about that. Most of us go too far in the other direction by setting our sights too low.

6. *Keep your affirmations visible in your life.* Plaster them on the walls of your bedroom, in your kitchen, or in the office, and keep them in your purse or wallet. Let them seep into every aspect of your life until they finally *are* a part of you.

7. *Use repetition.* State the affirmations you have set down for yourself over and over, regularly and consistently. The more frequently you go to your level and plug in the kinds of things you want to happen in your life, the faster you will attain them. Bombard yourself with mental suggestions. After all, throughout your life you have been bombarded with ideas and opinions that you have had little control over. You are now striving to counteract that effect. Almost immediately you will begin to notice the difference.

8. *Shelve negative thoughts that creep in.* Use "thought stoppage." Command yourself to stop at the onset of any self-defeating, destructive thoughts. But always give yourself an out. Keeping control of

your thoughts does not come easy at first. Angry, resentful, hostile, or negative ideas will push their way in until the new thoughts have been firmly established. And you will sometimes feel like giving in to debilitating past modes of thought. Unfortunately, once you begin to struggle with yourself, the battle is frequently lost. A better, easier way to handle this inner battle is to tell yourself, "All right, I'll go ahead and let myself feel hostile, rotten, angry, and negative, and think all the mean and nasty thoughts I want to. But not now. I'll set aside a time for it. Sunday afternoon, between three and four P.M., I'll give myself the luxury of letting loose my thoughts."

By doing this, you avoid the immediate struggle with yourself. You are telling yourself that you don't *have* to keep control of your thoughts *forever*—a task that sounds formidable. After a few days, you can go back to your old ways, if that's what you want to do. As it usually turns out, by the time Sunday arrives, you will have realized that you *can* be the master of your fate; you are beginning to see the benefits and have attained such a sense of power and control in your life, you *won't want* to fall back into old thought patterns.

Always avoid backing yourself into a corner where you feel you *have* to do or not do something. Give yourself an alternative. *There is nothing on earth that you have to do.* As soon as you fully realize this simple truth, you'll feel a sense of freedom and have the sustained desire to get on with those things that are important to your life.

Stage Three: Using mental imagery to maximize your success.

The final stage is to combine a heightened state of relaxation where you are highly susceptible to suggestion with visual mental imagery. Creation of the appropriate images during this state speeds up the change process.

Although the power of mental imagery has become more widely recognized in the past decade and is now included in many textbooks, popular works, and programs for change, it is far from new. Mental imagery was used by the yoga masters and dates back over eight hundred years.

Begin by letting your imagination come alive. Think of a situation in which you have already achieved some success. This need not be a major accomplishment, just some time in the past when you were at your best—a situation where you did an outstanding job or acquired something you wanted through your own efforts, or an event in your life that held special meaning for you. It might have been confronting some obstacle in your life that you were able to overcome or successfully circumvent.

Take a few minutes to reflect on past events in your life until you are able to recreate some of these success situations in the present moment. Focus on it and let it crystallize in your mind. As you do this, let your eyes close and enter into a deep state of relaxation where you are readily susceptible to new images as they flow into your consciousness.

Now project a blackboard or screen in your mind. This can be an ordinary, rectangular schoolroom blackboard or a large movie screen. Use your imagination to project yourself on the screen. This may not happen immediately. On their first attempt to create mental images of themselves, most people come up with fuzzy pictures. Facial expressions are especially hard to visualize.

If you have access to a video cassette player, by all means make use of it, and, if possible, have others present for the playback. Seeing yourself on video will aid you in becoming a more objective observer of yourself. And by exposing yourself on the screen to yourself and others, you receive important feedback. Most of us see ourselves in distorted ways. Video tape will give you a more realistic picture of yourself. This can aid you to greater self-acceptance. After a seminar in which I used video, one of the participants, a sixty-two-year-old woman, phoned the next day to tell me how excited she was about her video experience. Prior to the seminar, she had never seen herself on television, and thought of herself as "a tired old lady." During the seminar, she was filmed while happily relating one of her success images; her face was animated and her body posture reflected confidence and enthusiasm. *She had never realized that she looked so good.* This boost to her ego gave her a new radiance and zest for living. That night when she met her friends they told her she had never looked younger.

After you have observed yourself on video, you will find it easier to get a sharper, clearer image of yourself in your mind's eye.

Try these additional suggestions to crystallize your images:

1. Use color. With your eyes closed and comfortably relaxed, visualize the specific clothes and adornments you are wearing on your mental screen: shirt or blouse, slacks, skirt, tie, or scarf. Try to *see* the stripes, dots, prints, and colors of your clothes. See the gold or

Visualizing for success

silver jewelry, the painted nails, the bright lips, and the hazel eyes. Is
your skin vibrant or pale? What color are your shoes? How does your
hair look?

2. *Visualize objects and forms.* Now add some simple shapes to the
screen. Suggest a triangle, a suitcase, a fruit, a plant, or a flower to
yourself. Keep them in color. Picture yourself carrying the suitcase,
eating an orange, or watering a plant. See yourself fondling a fistful of
green, crumpled $1,000 bills. Get a clear picture in your mind. Then
mentally experience *touching* the bills. *Hear* the sound as they crum-
ple between your fingers and in your palm. *Smell* the scent given off.
You might even imagine how they might *taste* if you ran your tongue
along one of the bills. *Get all of your senses involved* and the impact
will be stronger.

3. *Add movement.* Picture yourself acting out different roles on the
screen. See yourself moving about: stretching, dancing, talking and
laughing. Visualize maintaining a confident, relaxed, happy posture.
Project yourself on the screen the way you want to be—creative,
committed, positively moving toward the kinds of successes you
desire.

4. *Dramatize your past successes.* Again, run through your past and
focus on a situation in which you were successful. Take in all the
sights and sounds of the situation. Let yourself go completely into
that setting. How do you feel? What emotions are dominant? How do
you act? What kind of expression is on your face? How do you carry
yourself? Are you alone or with others? The aim is to amplify and
expand on this past success, to see and experience yourself vividly
and clearly. As you blow up and relive this event, you can carry it into
the present and relate it to your ongoing desires and wishes.

5. *Awake and step into the success image.* Finally, open your eyes
and attempt to step into that image. Actually take on the success
characteristics of the person in your mind's eye.

In practicing your visualizations, continue to use the principles of
informational input you learned in the last section: work on only one
success category at a time, always see yourself in positive terms, get
all your senses involved, and use repetition. Don't forget to precede
your visualizations with one of the means for heightened relaxation,
such as breathing exercises or self-hypnosis. The deeper the state you
can attain, the quicker the changes will come about.

Color-Shape Coding

Another strategy to speed up the change process is Color-Shape
Coding. Think of a favorite color, and put a shape of this color across

the top of the screen in your mind. It can be round like an orange or the sun. It can be a square, a diamond, or a triangle.

After you get your success images down pat, back up and visualize the Color-Shape *immediately before* visualizing the success image. Then, in the future, as soon as you flash on that color and shape, the success image will follow automatically.

What you are doing is mentally tying a color-shape to your mental success image in order to more quickly and effortlessly call up the images you desire.

This technique can be used with all of your success visualizations. First, decide on the success image you are ready to program for. Let's say it is a Pacific cruise. Next, select an appropriate color and shape to be used *only* with that image. Perhaps in this case you would choose a deep blue color to represent the soothing waters of the Pacific, and an oblong shape like an island. Any color and shape can be used, but select ones that you feel easily lend themselves to the image you're practicing. Stay away from any shapes that are too complex. Also be sure that the color-shapes you condition to your separate success images are distinct and different enough from one another so as not to call up the wrong mental picture.

If you find yourself drawing a blank in trying to recall past personal successes, bring a model onto the screen—someone you know or whom you have observed achieving the kinds of things you desire. Then see yourself imitating his or her modes of response, as an outstanding public speaker, at ease with the opposite sex, as a pro tennis player, full of energy, decisive, and so on. Do not blindly imitate them, but adapt these responses in a way that feels natural for you.

Timothy Gallwey, author of the best-seller *The Inner Game of Tennis*, found that when he suggested to his trainees that they were one of the pro tennis players such as Billie Jean King, their game improved remarkably.[2]

Sometimes as you are going through scenes in your mind and trying to create success images, failure scenes will jump out at you instead—just what you don't want. A simple and effective means of handling this is to construct a mental eraser—a big black eraser to wipe them out. Here's how: Close your eyes and picture a blackboard. Now visualize an eraser at the top of the board. Picture this going back and forth, back and forth, down the board until the failure scene

---

2. *T. Gallwey,* The Inner Game of Tennis *(New York: Random House, 1974).*

is completely erased and the board is black again. This can take less than a second.

Going to your level, program in the statement: "Every time a failure scene attempts to make its way onto the screen, my eraser will automatically pop out on the screen and quickly, efficiently erase it." As elementary as this procedure sounds, it works.

How mental imagery works

Just as the thoughts dominant in our minds determine our actions, the images we dwell upon reflect who we are and can be powerful instigators of behavior. Consider how erotic pictures in our minds arouse us sexually, or how a frightening image can cause our hearts to pound. One physiologist has demonstrated that if we vividly imagine ourselves jogging, the muscles we use in jogging will show a measurable amount of contraction.[3]

Creating an abundance of success images in your consciousness gives you a new source from which to draw in real-life situations. Instead of falling back on former failure images that have been programmed in by chance, you can call up the success image you have decided on. For example, if you have been plagued with a series of illnesses or health problems recently, go to your level and think back to the healthiest and happiest period of your life. Let this image crystallize in your mind; feel the warm glow of a germ-free body, the fresh energy and the vibrant spark of life within you. Now bring this image into the present, focusing on it until you can see it clearly. You are a healthy, whole person, feeling younger and more radiant than ever before.

Perhaps you have had a string of business failures or financial disasters and have started to see yourself as someone who can't do anything right. Again, deeply relax and project a screen in your mind. Drift back in time to when you made a business decision that you were proud of. Feel the joy of success. You encountered many obstacles, but you persevered to come out on top. Dwell on this image and enter into it now. Make it a part of today. You are an astute business person. You have a good sense of what to do and what not to do in your investments. Counteract any failure images invading your consciousness with this success image. Use the eraser technique to quickly get rid of any negative self-images that crop into your mind.

---

3. E. Jacobson, Progressive Relaxation (Chicago: University of Chicago Press, 1942).

Maybe your personal relationships have been out of whack lately; nothing seems to be working out the way you hoped it would. You're discouraged and down on yourself, and you have been feeding on thoughts and images that are only perpetuating the situation. Make a decision to take charge of those movies-of-the-mind. Relax and remember your first youthful romance: the tender kiss, the warm love and energy that engulfed your body. Allow that affection to flow into your life in the present moment. Visualize yourself as the empathic and loving person that you are; see others responding in kind. Know that you can be and have whatever you ardently desire.

Preconscious strategies and Scimode

The strategies discussed in this chapter are to be used in conjunction with those outlined earlier. Conscious modes of thought and preconscious strategies complement each other; Scimode and mental imagery go hand in hand. Through careful observations and the use of your Time-Reactor-Log, you develop links that give you greater predictive power. You can then set up the events in your life to your best advantage. With mental imagery, you build a portfolio of success pictures from which to draw. Go back to past successes and recreate the experiences in the present, thereby reinforcing what you were doing right. Focusing on these positive images in a deeply relaxed, sensitive state, you allow them to seep into every part of your present consciousness. Finally, all you need do is step into the image in real life, bringing success to action in your day-to-day living.

V.
EPILOGUE

In making use of the ideas presented here, remember that the road to success is not always smooth, but has its peaks and troughs. Yet in spite of intervening obstacles, success will come if the ultimate direction has been clearly thought out and charted and you are using the appropriate procedures. Your commitment and follow-through are crucial. If you regularly and systematically live the suggestions that have been outlined, you will begin to see changes taking place almost immediately. Within thirty to ninety days, you'll see definite, even dramatic results.

Decide today to take time for leisure and let more success flow into your life.

Resource Directory

Selected newsletters, books, and cassette tapes to help you achieve continued success

Newsletters

Physical Fitness-Health

Executive Fitness Newsletter. Rodale Press, Inc., 33 East Minor St., Emmaus, PA 18049. Biweekly. $24 yr.

The Health Letter. Communications, Inc., P.O. Box 326, San Antonio, TX 78292. Bimonthly. $19.50 yr.

Time Management

Execu Time: The Newsletter on Effective Use of Executive Time. MRH Associates, Inc., P.O. Box 11318, Newington, CT 06111. Monthly. $36 yr.

Time Talk. Time Management Center, P.O. Box 5, Grandville, MI 49418. Monthly. $29 yr.

Vacation/Travel

The Joyer Travel Report. Phillips Publishing, Inc., 7315 Wisconsin Ave., Washington, D.C. 20014. Monthly. $36 yr.

Success as an Investor and Consumer

Bottom Line/Personal. Bottom Line Information, Inc., 500 Fifth Ave., New York, N.Y. 10110. Bimonthly. $39.95 yr.

Sound Advice: The English & Cardiff Real Estate & Investment Advisory Letter. P.O. Box 487, Walnut Creek, CA 94596. Monthly. $125 yr.

Towers Club USA Newsletter. Towers, P.O. Box 2038, Vancouver, WA 98668. Monthly. $46 yr.

Books

Leisure for Fun, Creativity, and Profit

Csikszentmihalyi, M. *Beyond Boredom and Anxiety*. San Francisco: Jossey Bass, 1975.

Gentz, Marvin C. *What To Do While Waiting*. Berkeley, CA: The Press of Time, 1977.

Hardy, C. C. *Dun & Bradstreet's Guide to Your Investments*. New York: Thomas Y. Crowell. Published annually.

Leckart, B. *Up From Boredom, Down From Fear*. New York: R. Marek Publishers, 1980.

Lefkowitz, B. *Breaktime: Living Without Work in a Nine to Five World*. New York: Hawthorn Books, 1979.

Levinson, J. C. *Earning Money Without a Job*. New York: Holt, Rinehart & Winston, 1979.

McCullagh, J. C., ed. *Ways to Play*. Emmaus, PA: Rodale Press, 1978.

Pollock, T. *Managing Yourself Creatively*. New York: Hawthorn Books, 1971.

Prosser, D. C. *Peel Your Own Onion*. New York: Everest House, 1979.

Ross, M. H. *Creative Loafing: A Shoestring Guide to New Leisure Fun*. San Diego: Comn Great, 1979.

Sackson, Sid. *Beyond Competition*. New York: Pantheon Books, 1977.

Waitley, D. *The Winner's Edge*. New York: Times Books, 1980.

Weiskopf, D. *A Guide to Recreation and Leisure*. Boston: Allyn & Bacon, 1975.

Yee, M. S., and Wright, D. K., Eds. *The Great Escape: A Source Book of Delights and Pleasures for the Mind and Body*. New York: Bantam Books, 1974.

Especially for the Workaholic

Hansel, T. *When I Relax I Feel Guilty*. New York: Cook, 1979.

Levinson, H. *Executive Stress*. New York: Harper & Row, 1975.

Oates, W. E. *Workaholics, Make Laziness Work for You*. New York: Abingdon, 1979.

Nutrition, Health, Well-Being

Airola, Paavo. *Are You Confused?* Phoenix: Health Plus Publishers, 1971.

Ardell, D. B. *High Level Wellness*. Emmaus, PA: Rodale Press, 1977.

Hayden, N. *Everything You Always Wanted To Know About Energy But Were Too Weak To Ask*. New York: Pocket Books, 1977.
Jones, Susan S. *The Main Ingredients: Positive Thinking, Exercise & Diet*. Provo, Utah: BiWorld Publishers, 1978.
Spino, Dyveke. *New Age Training for Fitness and Health*. New York: Grove Press, 1979.

Relaxation

Bedford, Stewart. *Stress & Tiger Juice*. Chico, CA: Scott Publications, 1980.
Benson, Herbert. *The Relaxation Response*. New York: Avon Books, 1975.
Teplitz, J. *How to Relax and Enjoy . . .* Tokyo: Japan Publications, 1977.
Walker, C. E. *13 Ways To Reduce Tension*. Englewood Cliffs, N.J.: Prentice-Hall, 1975.

Vacations and Weekends

Gunther, Max. *The Weekenders*. New York: Lippincott, 1964.
Shapiro, S. A., and Tuckman, A. J. *Time Off: A Psychological Guide to Vacations*. New York: Doubleday, 1978.

Retirement

Downs, H. and Roll, R. J. *The Best Years Book*. New York: Delacorte Press, 1981.
Hills, L. Rust. *How To Retire at 41: Dropping out of the Rat Race Without Going Down the Drain*. New York: Doubleday, 1973.
Neuhaus, Ruby H., and Neuhaus, Robert H. *Successful Aging*. New York: John Wiley & Sons, 1982.

Time Management

Bliss, E. C. *Getting Things Done*. New York: Bantam Books, 1976.
Ellis, A. and Knaus, W. J. *Overcoming Procrastination*. New York: Institute for Rational Living, 1977.
Goldfein, D. *Everywoman's Guide to Time Management*. Millbrae, CA.: Les Femmes Publishing, 1977.
Lakein, A. *How To Get Control of Your Time and Your Life*. New York: New American Library, 1973.
LeBoeuf, M. *Working Smart*. New York: McGraw-Hill, 1979.

Love, S. F. *Mastery and Management of Time.* Englewood Cliffs, NJ:
Prentice-Hall, 1978.
Mackenzie, R. A. *The Time Trap.* New York: McGraw-Hill, 1972.
McCay, J. T. *The Management of Time.* Englewood Cliffs, NJ: Prentice-
Hall, 1973.

Meditation/Imagery

Maltz, Maxwell. *The Magic Power of Self Image Psychology.* Engle-
wood Cliffs, NJ: Prentice-Hall, 1964.
Powers, Melvin. *A Practical Guide to Self-Hypnosis.* No. Hollywood,
CA: Wilshire Book Co., 1976.

For Further Study

Anderson, N. *Man's Work and Leisure.* Leiden, Netherlands: Brill,
1974.
Burenstom Linder, S. *The Harried Leisure Class.* New York: Columbia
University Press, 1970.
De Grazia, S. *Of Time, Work and Leisure.* New York: Anchor Books,
1960.
Ellis, M. J. *Why People Play.* Englewood Cliffs, NJ: Prentice-Hall, 1973.
Glasser, R. *Leisure: Penalty or Prize?* London: Macmillan, 1970.
Kelly, J. *Leisure.* Englewood Cliffs, N.J.: Prentice-Hall, 1980.
Marrus, M. R., ed. *The Emergence of Leisure.* New York: Harper &
Row, 1974.
Neulinger, J. *The Psychology of Leisure.* Springfield, Ill.: C. C. Thomas,
1974.
Neulinger, J. *To Leisure: An Introduction.* Boston: Allyn & Bacon,
1981.
Parker, S. *The Future of Work and Leisure.* New York: Praeger, 1971.
Veblen, T. B. *The Theory of the Leisure Class.* New York: Mentor Books,
1953.
Whitrow, G. J. *The Nature of Time.* London, England: Thames &
Hudson, 1972.

Books on Tape

Books on Tape, Box 7900, Newport Beach, CA 92660.
Classic & modern favorites including current best-sellers. Write for
catalog of books or call toll-free (800) 854-6758; in California
(800) 432-7646.

Audio-Cassette Tapes

Relaxation, Health, Well-Being   Source*

Basic relaxation & ego-strengthening program	(L)
Letting go of stress	(A)
Deep relaxation	(M)
Health & wellness	(A)
Visualization	(E)
Healing journey	(A)

Controlling Excesses

Smoke no more	(A)
Lose weight	(D)
Imagine yourself slim	(A)
Stop drinking	(M)
Stop nail biting	(B)
Relax & reduce	(J)
Stop smoking/Control drinking	(N)

Emotional Upbeat

Stop being angry	(B)
Jealousy	(B)
Up from depression	(B)
Increase your confidence & self-esteem	(D)
Developing enthusiasm	(M)
Self-confidence	(M)
How to be happy	(M)
Overcoming worry	(M)
Self-image programming	(M)

Success and Prosperity

Decision-making	(M)
Memory	(M)
Subconscious sales power	(B)
Goal setting	(N)
How to attract money	(M)
Developing your creativity	(M)

*See p. 145

Fear of success   (F)
How to become financially independent   (K)

Improve Your Sports Abilities

Be a better bowler   (F)
How to be a great golfer   (B)
Tennis   (B)
Baseball   (F)
Running free   (A)

Relationships

Attracting more love   (M)
Attract—Improve relationships   (D)
Get more joy out of sex   (B)
Divorce   (F)
Loss of a loved one   (B)
Improving relationships (old & new)   (M)

Sleep

The sleep tape (putting the day to rest; escape from
  insomnia)   (A)
Restful, revitalizing sleep   (M)

Meditation Music

Rainbow
  butterfly   (Georgia Kelly, Emmet Miller)   (A)
Birds of paradise   (Harp and flute music)   (F)
Golden voyage   (Ron Dexter)   (H)
Tarashanti   (Georgia Kelly)   (F)
Ancient echoes   (Steven Halpern and Georgia Kelly) (F)
Seapeace   (Georgia Kelly)   (F)
You are the ocean   (Schawkie Roth)   (O)

Retirement

Slowing down the aging process   (I)
Successful retirement   (F)

*Sources of Cassette Tapes

(A) Tapes
Emmett E. Miller, M.D.
P.O. Box W
Stanford, CA 94305

(B) Potentials Unlimited
4808 Broadmoor
Grand Rapids, MI 49508

(C) SRI Records
P.O. Box 1584
Palo Alto, CA 94302

(D) The Randolph Tapes
Box 178477
San Diego, CA 92117

(E) Autogenic Training
2510 Webster St.
Berkeley, CA 94705

(F) Rockwater Tapes
P.O. Box 5861
Santa Fe, NM 87502

(G) Biomonitoring Applications, Inc.
270 Madison Ave.
New York, NY 10016

(H) Awakening Productions
4132 Tuller Ave.
Culver City, CA 90230

(I) Total Mind Power Institute
San Francisco Regional Center
5 Bon Air Road
Larkspur, CA 94939

(J) Creative Imaging Associates
P.O. Box 95
Newton, MA 02158

(K) Success Motivation Institute
P.O. Box 7614
Waco, TX 76710

(L) Nathaniel Branden
     The Biocentric Institute
     9255 Sunset Blvd.
     Los Angeles, CA 90069

(M) Effective Learning Systs.
     6950 France Ave. So. #14
     Edina, MN 55435

(N) Valley of the Sun
     Box 38
     Malibu, CA 90265

(O) Heavenly Music
     P.O. Box 1063
     Larkspur, CA 94939

Audio-Cassette Rentals

Discovery Cassette Exchange
P.O. Box 105
Richmond, MO 64085
Telephone (816) 776-2664

Sells and rents cassette tapes on personal development, prosperity, motivation, goal-setting, health, and much more.